A BLANC CHRISTMAS
RAYMOND BLANC

—

'*Raymond Blanc is the most talented person cooking in this country.*'
Observer

*I*n *his new book, Raymond Blanc, Britain's most celebrated chef, presents his ideas on foods and decorations for a perfect Christmas celebration. In twelve spectacular menus, he describes how to prepare and cook a variety of meals, which are interspersed with chapters on mouthwatering canapés, cakes for afternoon tea, edible gifts, petits fours and accompaniment vegetables. The atmosphere of the book is also rich in memories of simpler celebrations in the France of his childhood, of more recent festivities enjoyed amidst the splendours of his renowned hotel-restaurant, Le Manoir aux Quat' Saisons. The recipes are well within the competence of the home cook, and are all imbued with Raymond Blanc's own extraordinary personality and flair. With a front cover portrait of Raymond Blanc by the Earl of Lichfield, and illustrated throughout with superb colour photographs of food, table settings and seasonal decorations by Peter Knab, this book is a must for every creative Christmas cook.*

A BLANC CHRISTMAS

RAYMOND BLANC

HEADLINE

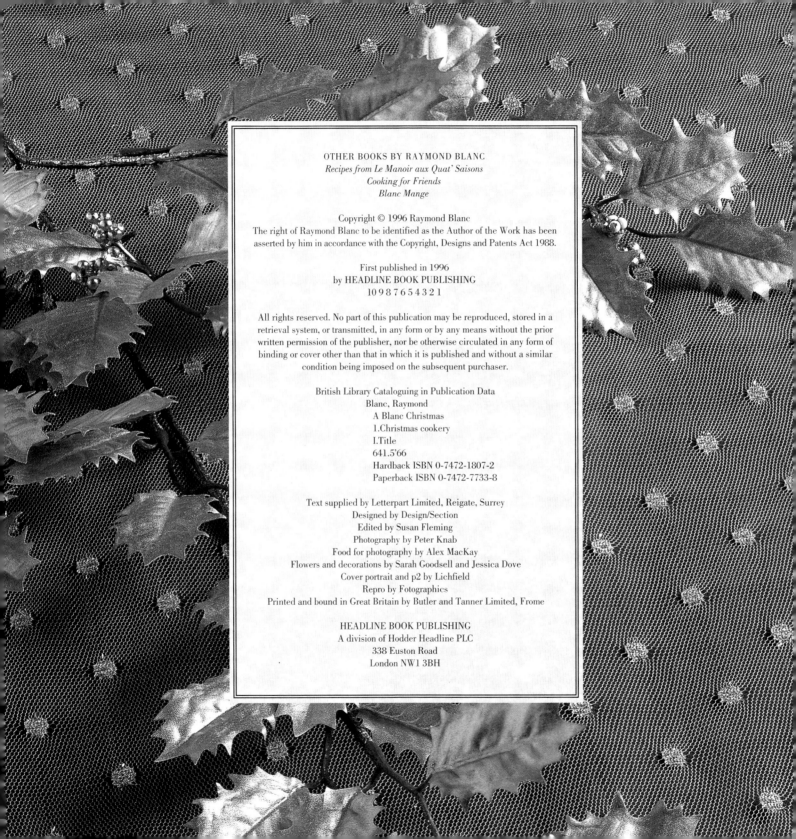

OTHER BOOKS BY RAYMOND BLANC
Recipes from Le Manoir aux Quat' Saisons
Cooking for Friends
Blanc Mange

First published in 1996
by HEADLINE BOOK PUBLISHING
10 9 8 7 6 5 4 3 2 1

British Library Cataloguing in Publication Data
Blanc, Raymond
A Blanc Christmas
1.Christmas cookery
I.Title
641.5'66
Hardback ISBN 0-7472-1807-2
Paperback ISBN 0-7472-7733-8

Text supplied by Letterpart Limited, Reigate, Surrey
Designed by Design/Section
Edited by Susan Fleming
Photography by Peter Knab
Food for photography by Alex MacKay
Flowers and decorations by Sarah Goodsell and Jessica Dove
Cover portrait and p2 by Lichfield
Repro by Fotographics
Printed and bound in Great Britain by Butler and Tanner Limited, Frome

HEADLINE BOOK PUBLISHING
A division of Hodder Headline PLC
338 Euston Road
London NW1 3BH

CONTENTS

—

INTRODUCTION

I love Christmas. And if it is a *blanc* - or white - Christmas, I love it even more, as it reminds me of all my family Christmases: the smells, the excitement, the beautiful food, the presents....Growing up in Besançon, Christmas was always white. The surrounding magnificent Jura mountains stood gleaming under a metre-thick blanket of snow, and the cold nights would send us rushing for our blankets and huge frothy winter eiderdowns, the work of our loving grandmother. For at that time none of the houses in our village enjoyed central heating, leading to picturesque frosted windows and icicles - and making the dash from kitchen fire to warmed beds a fierce competition between my two brothers, two sisters and myself.

Somehow, competition and argument always reared their ugly heads during the season of peace and goodwill. The silky slopes and hills allowed skiing and sledging from far above the village right through to the last house. By the time my friends and I reached the bottom, there would be a handful of bruises, scrapes, sprained toes and some very upset dogs, snatched from neighbours' doorsteps as we passed by. Inevitably, my brothers and I would be singled out as the chief troublemakers, much to my religious mother's embarrassment. Then for several days afterwards we would be seen, pink-faced, scrubbed and chastened, trailing alongside her to each church service, as she prayed for our atonement several times daily.

If I was far more often at fault than either of my brothers, Gerard and Michel, I think they will concede that I was just as often at the centre of Christmas fun and revelry. As a child I longed to be master of the celebrations, to show my family how much - despite my naughtiness - I loved them. One advantage of my numerous punishments was being made to stay indoors and observe my mother, intent on her mysterious culinary tasks and preparations: the *boudin blanc*, the plucked goose, the Bûche de Noël and the delicate *papillotes*, sweets or chocolates twisted into colourful cellophane. I determined to know her secrets, particularly the last - the sight and sound of those stiff, crackling packages became my most enduring Christmas memory. As we belonged to a working-class background, the wrapped presents, Christmas stockings and *papillotes* rarely revealed extravagant contents, but all that mattered was the expectation, the intricate preparation of carefully designed parcels and exquisitely stitched stockings, and the simple joy of giving to loved ones - even if it was only oranges and nuts.

One time in my childhood when I did very much succeed in being master of ceremonies (although only metaphorically speaking) was during the 1954 nativity play. We Blancs as a bunch are small of stature, and although way past infancy, I was cast as Baby Jesus, the Lord of Christmas. Squashed into a makeshift crib, resplendent in my aunt's satin curtains, I was pleased to be the centre of everyone's attention at last. We were praised for our tableau during Advent services, and all went well until the all-important

Christmas Eve celebration. My brother Michel played Joseph, a role that suited him very well. Michel is extremely conscientious, the nicest person I know, and he assiduously acted out the part. Unfortunately, the sudden realisation that for a while I was representing Jesus was a little bit too much to stomach, and I broke into irrepressible bursts of laughter. I was unable to stop giggling throughout the service, despite Michel's frowns and desperate pinches. He was the grumpiest Joseph I had ever seen. This little escapade was to cost me twenty Hail Maries, and what seemed like an hour on bended knee.

In France, Christmas is celebrated both as a religious festival and a family feast. The festivities would start right after Midnight Mass. The men, who did not go to church, would stay at home playing cards. The women, coming back from church, would start cooking and preparing food for their men, whilst the children would be sent promptly to bed. This evening was known as the *réveillon*.

We children had an early start on the morning of the 25th. The sight of gleaming presents under the tree was every child's joy, and the taste of those hand-made *papillotes* remains memorable. Then lunchtime was a big occasion. The table would never sit less than twenty people. After my mother said Grace, uncles, aunts, grandfathers, cousins, etc, would all join in a huge family celebration. My mother was the mistress of ceremonies, and presented us with no less than eight or ten courses. Usually oysters would come first, followed by trays of the French favourite - *escargots* - then a terrine followed by the traditional goose; we would then go on to a huge tray of cheeses, a choice of salads,

WELCOME DOOR RING
Buy or make a ring out of willow strands (these must be fresh; tie them together with either florists' wire or string). Bind some ribbon around the willow frame, leaving gaps, to make it look interestingly uneven. Decide now where you wish to place your decoration, at one side, at the foot, at the top, or all around. Glue or wire fresh or artificial foliage into place, then finish with baubles, fruit, bells, bunches of grapes, cones etc.

and the Bûche de Noël and Iles Flottantes....All this was accompanied by the best Burgundy wines.

By the time we reached the cheese course, the men were exultant and, as usual at Christmas, the old war stories would be dragged out. Again as expected, the men became sentimental and nationalistic. One particular Christmas, however, we children had had enough, and after almost an hour of listening to Papa's impassioned tedium, I dared to remind him that despite our brave efforts, we French had actually succumbed to the Germans, and that without British and American help we would still be under Germany's heel. To make it worse, I also suggested that many a great Frenchman had collaborated with the Nazis during the Occupation. His wrath and that of my uncles (who had also fought in the war), was overwhelming and immediate. Phlegm, fists and plates flew as they scolded my treacherous impudence, and only after the sublime Bûche de Noël, accompanied by my mother's wails, hit the ceiling, did the uproar cease. That Christmas was extremely hilarious.

Now, having (almost) grown up, and as chef and patron of Le Manoir aux Quat' Saisons, my hotel and restaurant in Oxfordshire, I have shared this magical time of Christmas with many friends, and am continually thrilled at the wonderful opportunity to give so much pleasure. The British actually celebrate Christmas with far more pomp and splendour than the French, and I have happily taken advantage of this at Le Manoir. Every year we go to town, decorating doors with welcome rings of foliage, spangles, baubles and bows, and with a magnificent Christmas tree in the entrance hall. The house is awash with flowers, and harpists, choristers and Champagne greet our guests. Christmas is a time when our guests are particularly at ease and relaxed; they get up late in the morning, and come down to the lounge still in their dressing gowns, to be welcomed by a roaring fire beside which they open their presents....A magical moment.

The food we serve at Le Manoir at this time is both traditional and innovative, but always celebratory, and in this little book I have recreated some of these ideas, interspersed with more traditional British and French menus.

I like to think that my years in England have turned me into a better Frenchman, making me less rude, less chauvinistic and so on. But at a New Year demonstration in Alsace a few years ago, it appeared that I had perhaps become even more English than the English. I had forgotten about the ability of the French to immerse themselves in total, sensual enjoyment. As I was preparing to leave for England, a huge party was being organised, and I had no choice but to stay. Several of the culinary stars of France were still there - among them Guy Savoie, Alain Chapel, Michel Guerard - and the company of fifteen also included a Dutch tenor, a titled lady, a lady mayor, and several local butchers. (Never in England would one have dared to gather together such a diversity of classes.) Only after several hours did I feel able to share the same spirit shown by my companions - singing, drinking wonderful Alsace wines, eating, laughing, arguing. I had also forgotten that the French make combat, not conversation! It wasn't until they started to sing nationalistic songs (don't we all at some time in a long evening?), that I allowed my national pride, despite years of English discipline, to burst forth in a spirited rendering of La Marseillaise.

An English table would have surrendered at this point, and retired. But the great wine-maker, Leon Bayer, suddenly decided we should continue merrymaking in his vineyards. (May I remind you that it was minus 15 degrees outside.) This we did, and there I witnessed the sublime sight of the titled lady holding up her skirts to dance, serenaded by eager butchers. Amidst these gaieties, I noticed M. Bayer kneeling amidst the frozen landscapes of his vines. In explanation he said, 'I'm praying for a frost so hard it will kill the grapes.' I was horrified. 'But Raymond,' he laughed, 'we've had so many good yields that another great year will devalue all our wines.'

He was quite unrepentant when we all met for lunch the next day - a relatively sober affair that ended at three, so we were able to pack up our belongings and hangovers and leave for home. And, thanks to my friends' ministrations, this time I really did enter England a better - and truer - Frenchman.

Joyeux Noël.

ACKNOWLEDGEMENTS

Firstly I must thank Alex MacKay, a gifted young New Zealand chef, who has worked with me before, and who has recently returned to help as course director of L'Ecole de Cuisine. He has assisted me in developing the recipes, and coped with the cooking and styling of food for the photography.

I am also immensely grateful to Sarah Goodsell and Jessica Dove. Sarah is in charge of the flowers at Le Manoir, and she designed the arrangements, Christmas rings, swags and garlands in the book. Jessica runs Partymania in Oxford, and her party-organising skills were the inspiration for the table decorations, from cloths to bows to baubles! She also kindly lent us her house for a day's shooting. Much appreciation to Soma Ghosh for helping me with the introductions and for correcting my English.

The wonderful photographs of food and decorations are by Peter Knab, ably assisted by Nigel James. Peter calmly got on with it amidst a modicum of chaos in a variety of locations; he was a tower of strength. Peter's wife, Diana, also helped us find some of the many props. I am also very grateful to the Earl of Lichfield, for the portrait on the front of the book. All the photographs are stunning.

At Le Manoir, Elena Giacomelli, my assistant, has been coordinating the whole book operation, as well as running my working life. A big, big thank-you to her, and also to Clive Fretwell and Benoît Blin for their expertise and ability to answer all manner of questions. I owe an enormous debt of gratitude to my prize-winning sommelier, Henri Chapon, for all the wine suggestions. He has an unerring palate, and encyclopaedic knowledge of his subject.

I should also like to thank Felicity Bryan, my agent, who allowed her beautiful house to be invaded for a day's photography. At Headline, Susan Fleming, Liz Allen, Alan Brooke and Design/ Section have contributed their various expertises.

Many thanks to **Villeroy & Boch** for lending us all the glorious china. We thank **Waitrose** for having given us most of the ingredients.

All the recipes have been tested by ex-students of **Le Manoir cookery school**:
Mrs P. Budd, Mrs D. Cave, Mr T.D. Dampney, Mr and Mrs I. Fogg, Mrs C. Haynes,
Dr A. Langrick, Mr and Mrs M. Lennard, Mr B. Pearson, Mrs S.D. Picket, Mr and Mrs T.J. Pitts.

CANAPÉS AND
APERITIFS

—

*Whether you are entertaining your neighbours or some
dear friends you have not seen in a while, an evening
of canapés and aperitifs gives you the opportunity to
offer some Christmas hospitality without breaking too
much into your family time.*

*In creating these canapés I have endeavoured to give
you a beautiful selection that is easily prepared, and
which captures at a glance and a nibble the essence of
the festive season. Even in the midst of your Christmas
preparations, you will be able to find time to make these
simple, but delicious, canapés (some of them well in
advance), and thus be able to spend some quality time
with your friends rather than stuck at your kitchen stove.
I have also given a couple of recipes from my mother's
extensive repertoire of aperitifs, so choose one of them.
Or offer some Champagne, perhaps with a purée of pear
and vanilla, or peach.*

*Make a selection of four or five canapés per person,
and present them attractively on platters. Scatter a few
bowls of olives, some plates of antipasti and Christmas
crackers around your living room. Put napkins in every
conceivable spot.*

CROÛTES WITH TAPENADE AND QUAIL'S EGG AND/OR PESTO AND GOAT'S CHEESE

*This recipe gives you more tapenade and pesto than
you will need, but both are able to be kept perfectly in the fridge
so long as you cover their surfaces well with oil.*

Makes 16 canapés

Planning ahead: *The tapenade and pesto
These can be made weeks in advance.
The croûtes These may be made a day or two before
needed, and kept in an airtight container.
The topping must be put on no more than 1 hour before,
or the croûtes will soften.*

16 slices baguette, cut slightly on the bias

FOR THE TAPENADE AND QUAIL'S EGG TOPPING:

50g stoned black olives

*2 anchovies, rinsed and
finely chopped*

40ml virgin olive oil

4 quail's eggs

paprika to garnish

FOR THE PESTO AND GOAT'S CHEESE TOPPING:

50g basil leaves and stalks

20g pine nuts

40ml olive oil

1 garlic clove, peeled

juice of 1 small lemon

*8 small slices of your preferred
goat's cheese*

salt and pepper

FOR THE CROÛTES

Preheat the oven to 140°C/275°F/Gas 1.

Bake the slices of baguette in the preheated oven until lightly
browned and completely dry, about 5 minutes. Set aside.

FOR THE TAPENADE AND QUAIL'S EGG TOPPING

Purée the olives, anchovies and olive oil to a rough paste, either
using a food processor or a mortar and pestle.

Cook the quail's eggs for 3 minutes in boiling water. Once
cooked, run under cold water until completely cold.

With a butter knife, spread the tapenade over eight of the
croûtes, but only covering half of each. Peel the quail's eggs,
rinse under cold water, then cut in half and place one on top of
each croûte on the opposite side to the tapenade. Sprinkle
paprika over to garnish.

Keep the leftover tapenade in a jar in the fridge, covered with
olive oil.

FOR THE PESTO AND GOAT'S CHEESE TOPPING

In a food processor or mortar and pestle, purée together the basil,
pine nuts, olive oil, garlic and lemon juice until you have a rough
paste. Season to taste.

Spread on to the remaining eight croûtes, and top with a slice
of goat's cheese.

Keep the leftover pesto in a jar in the fridge, covered with
olive oil.

VARIATIONS

These croûtes are completely neutral in flavour. You can there-
fore top them with whatever you desire. Pâté springs to mind, as
do Parma ham and melon, salmon tartare, cauliflower purée -
whatever you fancy.

RB'S NOTE

*Try and get the croûtes completely dry. This will keep them
crunchy under your topping for an hour or so.*

CRAB AND PINK GRAPEFRUIT TARTARE

This mixture is perhaps a little more reminiscent of summer than Christmas time, but its wonderful freshness provides a contrast to the richness of some of the other recipes.
You can use this mixture in several ways – in the tartelettes or lettuce leaves as suggested below, or perhaps even on croûtes (see page 12).

Makes 16 canapés

100g cooked white crab meat
1 large shallot, peeled and very finely chopped
3 segments pink grapefruit, chopped (eat the rest for breakfast)
6 coriander leaves, finely cut
salt and cayenne pepper

Mix all the ingredients together. Season to taste with salt and cayenne pepper.

CRAB AND GRAPEFRUIT TARTELETTES

Makes 8 canapés

½ quantity Crab and Pink Grapefruit Tartare (see left)
100g shortcrust pastry
8 large coriander leaves
1 segment pink grapefruit, thinly sliced widthways

Preheat the oven to 180°C/350°F/Gas 4.

Roll out the pastry on a floured work surface to about 3mm or less in thickness, and cut out small rounds with a pastry cutter or a small cup, cutting around the latter with a knife. Place these pastry circles inside small mouthful-sized tartelette moulds. Place another tartelette mould the same size inside and bake in the preheated oven for 10 minutes. Remove the tartelettes from the moulds whilst still hot, otherwise they will continue to cook.

To serve, insert a coriander leaf into each tartelette, top with the crab tartare, and garnish with the small wedges of pink grapefruit.

CRAB AND LETTUCE PACKET

Makes 8 canapés

4 large leaves iceberg or romaine lettuce, ribs removed,
cut in half, approx. 5-7cm square, blanched and refreshed
½ quantity Crab and Pink Grapefruit Tartare (see above left)

Drain the leaves between two cloths. Divide the crab between them and raise the sides. Twist into a purse shape, and press tightly. Serve.

CARAMELISED ONIONS IN NIÇOISE STYLE

This onion mixture forms the flavourful basis for two canapés, Pissaladière and Prawns with Caramelised Onions and Sesame. You can also put it in tartlets, or spread it on croûtes.

Makes 20 canapés

Planning ahead: *This mixture keeps extremely well, up to 3-4 days in the fridge.*

20ml groundnut oil
800g onions (600g peeled weight), peeled and finely sliced
2 garlic cloves, peeled and finely sliced
1 tablespoon caster sugar
salt and pepper

In a medium pan, heat the oil, then cook the onions and garlic with the sugar over a low heat until soft and transparent, about 10 minutes. Raise the heat and continue cooking until you have a dark brown caramel colour, about 3-5 minutes. Taste for seasoning.

PISSALADIÈRE

Makes 12 canapés

Planning ahead: *This can be cooked in advance, cut and then reheated. It is also very pleasant at room temperature.*

300g puff pastry, rolled to a rectangle approx. 30cm long, 10cm wide and 5mm thick, and chilled for 1 hour
1 egg, size 3, beaten
⅔ quantity Caramelised Onions in Niçoise Style (see above), cooled
4 anchovies
4 olives

Preheat the oven to 180°C/350°F/Gas 4.

Cut 4 x 1cm strips from the side of the pastry sheet then cut the remainder in half lengthways. Brush a little egg wash along each long side of each large sheet then attach a 1cm piece of pastry on each long side, making two little walls. Brush the tops of these walls with a little more egg wash.

Spoon the onion mixture down the middle of both pastry bases, being careful not to go over the walls. Cut each of the anchovies and the olives in half lengthways and use as decoration. Bake in the preheated oven for approximately 15 minutes. Cut each into 6 pieces.

RB'S NOTE

 The pastry must be well rested in the fridge, otherwise it will shrink.

PRAWNS WITH CARAMELISED ONIONS AND SESAME

You will need some toothpicks to shape the canapés.

Makes 8 canapés

8 prawns, shelled except for the tail
⅓ quantity Caramelised Onions in Niçoise Style (see above left), cooled
2 tablespoons sesame seeds
2 tablespoons sesame oil

Shape the prawns into crescents. Stuff the centre of each with a teaspoon of the onion mixture then press a toothpick through from head to tail so they keep their shape. Roll in the sesame seeds until completely coated. Pan-fry for 1 minute each side in the sesame oil, then drain on absorbent paper and serve.

Again, these may be prepared in advance and reheated but they must not be refrigerated.

VEGETABLE MIXTURE WITH ASIAN ACCENTS

An easy to prepare mixture full of fine individual flavours that are versatile enough to be used in many different ways (see below).

Makes 16 canapés

Planning ahead: *The mixture can be made 2 days in advance. Cover well and keep in the fridge.*

20ml grapeseed oil
1 tiny piece fresh root ginger, peeled and very finely diced
1 garlic clove, peeled and very finely diced
50g each of leek, celery and carrot, cut into as fine strips as possible
50g cucumber, cut into similar fine strips
30g beansprouts
1 tablespoon pumpkin seeds
1 teaspoon cornflour or arrowroot mixed with 1 teaspoon soy sauce

Heat the grapeseed oil in a medium frying pan or wok. Add the ginger and garlic and cook without colouring for 30 seconds. Add the leek, celery and carrot and stir-fry for approximately 4 minutes. Now add the cucumber, beansprouts and pumpkin seeds, and fry for a further 30 seconds before adding the cornflour and soy sauce to thicken. Cook for 30 seconds more, stirring constantly. Take the mixture out of the pan and leave to cool.

RB'S NOTE

Be sure to cook the mixture for a good 30 seconds after adding the cornflour, or the taste of the cornflour will overpower the rest.

PRAWNS IN CABBAGE

You will need eight wooden toothpicks for these prawns.

Makes 8 canapés

Planning ahead: *May be pan-fried 1 hour in advance, then reheated in the oven.*

8 large tiger prawns, shelled except for the tail
4 large cabbage leaves (Savoy)
salt
½ quantity Vegetable Mixture with Asian Accents (see left)
olive oil

Blanch the cabbage quickly in boiling salted water. Cut eight rectangles approximately 8cm long from the leaves. Push a toothpick lengthways through each of the prawns. Spread a teaspoonful of the vegetable mixture along each piece of cabbage. Place the prawns on top of each with the tail sticking out a little. Roll up and press tightly. Pan-fry in hot olive oil for 1 minute on each side.

RB'S NOTE

 Obviously you will have a fair amount of cabbage left, only having removed four leaves: include it as a garnish for your main course, either buttered or stuffed with some extra stuffing.

CHRISTMAS CRACKERS

Makes 8 canapés

Planning ahead: *May be three-quarters cooked 1-2 hours in advance, then reheated in the oven when needed.*

4 sheets of filo pastry
1 egg, size 3, beaten
½ quantity Vegetable Mixture with Asian Accents (see above)
16 fat chives, blanched for 10 seconds in boiling water and refreshed
1 tablespoon pumpkin seeds

Preheat the oven to 180°C/350°F/Gas 4.

Cut each sheet of filo pastry in two. Brush each filo piece with a little egg wash. Place a spoonful of the vegetable mixture towards the centre at the bottom of each, then roll into a cylindrical shape. Be sure to leave a little extra at the sides to tie.

Pinch the sides to make a Christmas cracker shape, tie with the chives and trim the ends. Brush with egg wash again, sprinkle with pumpkin seeds and bake in the preheated oven for 6 minutes.

PRUNE AND BACON ON PUFF PASTRY

The traditional name for prunes wrapped in bacon and baked is angels on horseback. Quite fitting, I think, for Christmas!

Makes 8 canapés

Planning ahead: *These can be frozen and then cooked from frozen. If you freeze them, however, you must rest the pastry in the fridge beforehand for half an hour or so. This lets the pastry relax before freezing, which is vital.*

8 prunes, pitted
8 rashers streaky bacon
200g puff pastry, rolled to 7-8mm thick, and left to rest for 30 minutes in the fridge
1 egg, size 3, beaten

Preheat the oven to 180°C/350°F/Gas 4.

Roll the prunes inside the rashers of bacon, and press them tightly together. Next brush the pastry with the beaten egg. Place the prunes at intervals along the pastry and, using their size as a guide, cut a leaf shape around each of them. Rest in the fridge for 30 minutes, then bake in the preheated oven for 6 minutes – the sides will have risen, and the pastry should be golden brown.

CHICKEN KEBABS

You will need eight wooden toothpicks for this canapé.

Makes 8 canapés

Planning ahead: *The kebabs may be cooked in advance, but since they need to be fully cooked, they will dry a little when reheated.*

1 small skinless chicken breast, approx. 70g, cut into 1cm cubes
16 tiny broccoli florets
2 large shallots, peeled and cut into 1cm cubes
juice of ½ lime

4 large sprigs coriander, finely chopped
peanut oil
cayenne pepper

Make the kebabs by alternating the chicken with the pieces of broccoli and shallot until the eight toothpicks are full. Now marinate them with the lime juice, coriander, 50ml of the peanut oil and a little cayenne pepper for at least 6 hours, and up to 36 hours.

When ready, heat a medium frying pan and heat 1 tablespoon oil. Drain the kebabs, then cook them for about 2 minutes on each side.

VARIATIONS

Again you can use just about anything, especially in summer, when you could ally prawns with roasted peppers, or mussels with cherry tomatoes and basil. In winter you could have small pieces of beef with wild mushrooms. It's up to you.

SURPRISE SALMON PARCEL

Smoked salmon is very useful at Christmas. These 'parcels' look very special.

Makes 8 canapés

Planning ahead: *These can be made a day in advance and refrigerated under clingfilm.*

8 slices smoked salmon, approx. 8cm square
1 hard-boiled egg, size 3, roughly chopped
2 teaspoons drained capers
4 sprigs flat-leaf parsley, chopped
1 small shallot, peeled and finely diced
salt and black pepper
juice of ½ lemon
16 fat chives, blanched for 10 seconds and refreshed

Mix the chopped egg with the capers, parsley, shallot, salt, black pepper and lemon juice.

Lay the slices of smoked salmon, shiny side down, on your work surface and place a spoonful of the egg mixture in the centre. Fold the slices over, making a square parcel. Tie the 'presents' up with 2 chives each.

VARIATIONS

The crab tartare on page 13 would be lovely as a surprise parcel filling, as would a mixture of cream cheese, apple and walnut, or diced cucumber and raw fennel, bound with a little mayonnaise. The fillings can be as varied as your imagination.

RB'S NOTE

 Don't put these under the Christmas tree or they will dry out!

CUCUMBER WITH GOAT'S CHEESE

Makes 16 canapés

Planning ahead: These can be made 6-8 hours in advance.

½ *large English cucumber*
50g fresh goat's cheese or cream cheese
8 walnuts, chopped, plus 4 for garnish, each cut in four
1 small bunch chervil, chopped except for 16 leaves for garnishing
salt and pepper

Slice the cucumber in half lengthways, and scoop out the seeds, leaving a hollow. Remove a small slice of the skin from the bottom so that the pieces of cucumber sit flat. Set aside.

Cut the removed slice of cucumber skin into small dice. Mix this with the goat's cheese, chopped walnuts and chervil. Season to taste with salt and black pepper. Fill the crevice in the cucumber with this and smooth into place with the back of a spoon. Cut each half cucumber piece into eight triangles. Decorate with the reserved pieces of walnut and the chervil.

VARIATIONS

Blue cheese could replace the goat's cheese, or you could fill the crevice with crab. If cucumbers are not to your taste, celery could be used.

GINGERED MULLED WINE

Makes about 2.5 litres

2 bottles hearty red wine (Chilean Cabernet Sauvignon, for instance)
1 litre water
100g caster sugar
2 cinnamon sticks
2 lemons, finely sliced
2 oranges, finely sliced
1 lime, finely sliced
4 bay leaves
2 cloves
50g grated fresh ginger, wrapped in a little muslin bag

Place all the ingredients in a suitable large saucepan, bring to the boil, then turn down the heat and simmer for 20 minutes.

Leave in the pan and, using a big ladle, serve hot in tall heat-proof glasses, preferably with handles.

GRAPEFRUIT WINE

Keep the flesh of the grapefruit and make into juice, or serve for breakfast in segments, or in a fruit salad. Blood oranges could replace grapefruits in this recipe.

Makes about 2 litres

200g peel and pith of grapefruit
200g caster sugar
2 bottles dry white wine

Chop the grapefruit peel and pith roughly. Mix with the sugar, and place in jars. Pour the white wine over the top, seal, and leave to macerate for a week.

To serve, strain into glasses.

MENU 1

This is the closest to a traditional British Christmas menu, starting with smoked salmon. I suggest that you serve the Christmas turkey with figs and cooked watercress, but no, I haven't done this just to shock; the combination is sublime. Don't worry if the cranberry butter appears to be lost during the cooking, as by that time it will have made its subtle contribution. Involve everyone in the ritual of serving: a slice of breast; a moist nugget of thigh; a fig plump to bursting....As a proud Frenchman I don't defect easily, but how I love this traditional Christmas pudding. I must admit, though, to adding a few less usual touches!

SMOKED SALMON
WITH ITS TRADITIONAL
ACCOMPANIMENTS

ROAST TURKEY
WITH STUFFED FIGS AND
WATERCRESS PURÉE

RAYMOND BLANC'S
CHRISTMAS PUDDING

SMOKED SALMON WITH ITS
TRADITIONAL ACCOMPANIMENTS

This should certainly need no detailed explanation.
Allow 100-150g of the finest Scottish smoked salmon per person.

chopped boiled egg
small capers
chopped onions
sweet Hungarian gherkins
horseradish cream
A black pepper
grinder is essential!

If you can acquire a whole side rather than pre-sliced salmon, it is lovely, and very much in the festive spirit to slice it at the table. (This will also warm you up for the turkey later.)

Serve a basket of some excellent brown bread or perhaps Russian rye bread with some good unsalted butter and, if you like, a selection of some of the accompaniments listed on the left:

WINE

For this most traditional
of dishes, smoked salmon
with many garnishes,
why not try at home
what many restaurants
used to offer when
drinking and driving laws
were not so stringent –
a small glass of very cold
vodka, either plain,
lemon scented or spiced.

COLOUR COORDINATION

With a silver and gold or black theme, you have a huge choice of effects. Try spray-painting an interestingly shaped branch or twig, stripped of its leaves, with silver paint, and fix it in earth in a pot. (Artificial, glycerined or fresh leaves on a branch or twig could be spray-painted as well.) You could hang baubles on it if liked (an alternative Christmas tree, see page 18), or you could arrange baubles on the table, on a plate or dish as above, or on any flat surface in the room. Use silver ribbon to tie the napkins, and try scattering gold and silver stars around the tablecloth.

CHRISTMAS PRESENTS

As part of the decorative theme, you could place little black and silver wrapped presents on the side plates. Tie them with silver and gold ribbon, and you could make a small arrangement on top, where the bow might be.

ROAST TURKEY WITH STUFFED FIGS AND WATERCRESS PURÉE

Serves 8-10 people generously

Planning ahead: The cranberry compote and butter *May be made up to 3 days in advance.*
The stuffing *May be made the day before, as could the watercress purée.*
The figs *Can be prepared a day early, and stuffed as the turkey goes in the oven.*
The turkey *Ask the butcher to prepare it for you, to chop up the neck etc. On the day, it can be cooked and left to rest in a warm place for 1-2 hours. Wrapped in foil it will retain its heat and moisture. This will give you plenty of time to make the gravy.*

1 x 5kg bronze turkey
salt and pepper
50ml groundnut oil
100g unsalted butter

FOR THE CRANBERRY
COMPOTE AND BUTTER:
400g cranberries
400g caster sugar
50ml water
100g unsalted butter

FOR THE STUFFING
AND FIGS:
16-20 fresh figs
600g coarse-textured
sausagemeat
150g dried figs,
roughly chopped
150g shelled walnuts,
roughly chopped
the liver from the turkey,
roughly chopped
150g breadcrumbs
1 egg, size 3
ground allspice

MAKING THE CRANBERRY COMPOTE AND BUTTER

In a deep saucepan, mix together the cranberries, sugar and water. Bring them slowly to the boil. Give a little stir, then simmer very gently for 1 hour. By this time most of the liquid will have evaporated and the cranberries will have sweetened. Set aside to cool.

Once cool, take one-quarter of the mixture and incorporate it with the butter. Reserve both.

PREPARING THE STUFFING AND FIGS

Cut a small slice from the bottom of the fresh figs so they sit flat. Cut off the tops two-thirds of the way up, and remove half of the interior. Set aside.

To make the stuffing, simply mix all of the ingredients together, adding the reserved flesh of the fresh figs. Season well with salt, pepper and allspice. (To check the seasoning, make a small patty with some of the stuffing. Pan-fry it and taste.)

COOKING THE WATERCRESS PURÉE

Melt the butter in a large deep pan, add the shal- lots and cook without colouring over a low heat until soft. Add the spinach and watercress and cook over a fierce heat, stirring frequently, for 2-3 minutes until it has all wilted. Add the cream, and boil to reduce it by half. Season the mixture well with salt and pepper, then set aside.

STUFFING AND COOKING THE TURKEY

Preheat the oven to 200°C/400°F/Gas 6.

Rub the interior of the turkey with all the cranberry butter. To stuff the turkey, put as much of the stuffing as possible into the neck cavity, then fold over the flap of skin. Now push the rest of the stuffing, except for about one-sixth, into the body cavity. Truss and season the turkey well whilst still on your work surface; if you season when in the roasting tray, the sauce will be too salty.

Chop up the neck of the turkey and put the pieces across your roasting tray. Pour the oil over these, then top with the turkey. Rub the butter all over and cover everything with tin foil.

Roast in the preheated oven for 1 hour 40 minutes in total. Remove the foil after 40 minutes, and turn the oven down to 180°C/350°F/Gas 4.

WINE

A Vendange Tardive
Pinot Gris from Alsace
will have enough body
and character to match
the turkey. Try Domaine
Zind-Humbrecht,
Hugel or Domaine
Schlumberger. The
semi-sweetness from
the late harvest picking
will complement the
'jamminess' of the figs.

Cook for a further 45 minutes, basting every 15 minutes.

During this time, stuff the figs with the remaining stuffing. Add them to the roasting tray for the final 15 minutes of the cooking time.

At the end of the cooking time, remove the turkey from the oven, then place both it and the figs on a large dish and cover them with foil. Keep in a warm place until needed.

MAKING THE GRAVY

Pour off most of the fat from the roasting tray. Heat the remainder and incorporate the flour. Add the water and, stirring all the time, bring to the boil. Add the brown chicken stock, bring back to the boil and simmer for about 2 minutes. Pass the gravy through a sieve into a saucepan, and season well to taste.

SERVING

Carve the turkey, giving each guest some white and some dark meat. Decorate each plate with the figs and the cranberry compote. Serve with the warmed watercress purée and gravy on the side.

RB'S NOTES

※ The watercress purée *If you are making this in advance, cool it down quickly over ice so that it does not discolour.*

※ The turkey *You may be a little concerned about the cooking time (or lack of it). Believe me, it has been tried, tested and tried again. But you have your own oven, and your turkey may be chilled or at room temperature before going into the oven. Test by inserting a skewer or roasting fork into the thickest part of the thigh; if the liquid that comes out is transparent and not bloody, the turkey is cooked.*

FOR THE WATERCRESS PURÉE:

50g unsalted butter

8 large shallots, peeled and finely chopped

600g spinach, picked, washed and finely chopped

400g watercress, picked, washed and finely chopped

200ml whipping cream

FOR THE GRAVY:

1 tablespoon plain flour

100ml water

400ml Brown Chicken Stock (see page 76)

RAYMOND BLANC'S CHRISTMAS PUDDING

Fills 2 x 1 litre pudding basins or 1 x 2 litre basin

Planning ahead: The pudding(s) *Can be made 4-6 months in advance if kept in a cool dark place.*
The Armagnac butter *Can be made 1 or 2 days beforehand and chilled.*

250g each of raisins, currants, sultanas, brown breadcrumbs and brown sugar

75g nibbed almonds

1 Bramley apple, cored and finely chopped

grated zest and juice of 1 lemon and 1 orange

4 eggs, size 3, beaten

100g candied peel, chopped

50g wholemeal flour

1 teaspoon Chinese five-spice powder

100ml Armagnac

250g vegetable suet

FOR THE ARMAGNAC BUTTER:

150g unsalted butter

75g icing sugar

4-8 tablespoons Armagnac (depending on the spirit of Christmas you want)

TO SERVE:

Armagnac to flame

PREPARING THE PUDDING(S)

Prepare your basin(s) by greasing them well, with extra butter, then lining the bottom(s) with grease-proof paper.

In a large bowl mix all of the pudding ingredients together thoroughly.

Fill the pudding basin(s) to 1cm below the rim. Now cover with a circle of greaseproof paper followed by a larger piece of foil. Tie this around with a piece of string, but loosely so that there is room for the pudding to expand.

COOKING THE PUDDING(S)

Steam the larger pudding for 5 hours, the smaller ones for 3½-4 hours. If you do not have a steamer, cook the pudding(s) on a wire rack in a pan of boiling water. Make sure that the water boils constantly, and top it up occasionally.

Once cooked, remove the basin(s) from the steamer and leave to cool. Remove the pudding(s)

from the basin(s), wrap well with clean greaseproof paper, and store in a cool place until needed.

MAKING THE ARMAGNAC BUTTER

With an electric whisk cream the butter until white. Beat in the sugar gradually. Add the Armagnac little by little. Beat it in thoroughly, and should the mixture show any sign of curdling do not add all of the alcohol, as you can pour it over the top of the pudding when serving. The butter should be white and foamy. Refrigerate until needed.

REHEATING AND SERVING

Reheat the large pudding by steaming it for about 2 hours, 1 hour for the smaller ones. The longer you steam them, the darker they will become. Turn the pudding(s) out on to a serving dish, and decorate with some holly.

Heat and flame a ladleful of Armagnac, pour over the pudding and serve with the Armagnac butter separately.

VARIATION

You can use rum or brandy instead of the Armagnac in the pudding and in the butter.

*An entertaining mixture of the new and nostalgic.
The pâté is a great way to start, as it is the type of
dish that requires animated eating. The flavours that
follow with the salmon are honest and clear, as is the
simplicity of preparation. Steamed puddings are
relatively new to me, but I think this makes a lovely
variation on a traditional idea, the sweet-sour of the
cranberries complementing the fluffy sponge.*

SMOOTH CHICKEN LIVER
AND RAISIN PÂTÉ

POACHED SALMON
AND SHELLFISH WITH
SOFTENED LEEKS, BOK CHOY
AND FRESH PASTA

CRANBERRY STICKY TOPPED
STEAMED PUDDING

SMOOTH CHICKEN LIVER AND RAISIN PÂTÉ

Fills 5 x 150ml moulds

Planning ahead: This is an ideal beginning to a meal. It can be made up to 3 days in advance.

200g chicken livers, light in
colour, with all traces of
gall bladder and sinew removed

2 eggs, size 3

200g unsalted butter, melted
and slightly cooled

1 teaspoon salt

½ teaspoon ground white pepper

60g large raisins

FOR THE REDUCTION:

100ml white wine

100ml port

4 shallots, peeled and
finely sliced

1 garlic clove, peeled
and finely sliced

**FOR SEALING
THE PÂTÉ:**

50g clarified butter, melted

PREPARING THE REDUCTION

In a deep saucepan reduce the white wine and port with the sliced shallots and garlic until it is about a third of its original volume. Remove from the heat and pass through a fine sieve, pressing to extract the maximum of juice from the shallots. Set aside to cool.

MAKING THE PÂTÉ

In the bowl of a food processor or blender, purée the chicken livers until smooth. Add the port-wine reduction followed by the eggs, the melted butter than finally the salt and pepper. Pass through a fine sieve. Set aside.

COOKING THE PÂTÉ

Preheat the oven to 140°C/275°F/Gas 1.

Line up five round moulds. Small 7.5cm ramekins or oeufs sur plat dishes are ideal for this,

but tea cups (so long as they are ovenproof) will do. Divide the raisins between these moulds then pour the chicken liver mixture over. Leave a little space at the top of each mould.

Place the moulds into a deep tray, pour in enough cold water to reach two-thirds up the depth of the moulds, then cover with foil and cook in the preheated oven for 30-40 minutes. Check if the pâté is cooked. Push the blade of a small knife into the centre; if it comes out hot and dry the pâté is ready. If not quite firm enough, cook for a little longer.

Remove the pâté from the oven and from the bain-marie, then seal with the melted clarified butter to prevent discoloration. Leave to cool, then refrigerate until needed.

SERVING

Serve from the moulds, accompanied by some toast made from hazelnut or walnut bread and, if you so desire, a little salad dressed with walnut oil and wine vinegar.

VARIATION

You could put the raisins on top of the pâté once cooked, and glaze with the clarified butter.

RB'S NOTES

※ The reduction *The wine and port need to be reduced to intensify the flavours and to cook out the alcohol.*

※ Cooking the pâté *Be very careful with your oven temperature, as the pâté should be very smooth. If cooked at too high a temperature it will rise like a soufflé and then, once cold, become grainy and unpleasant. Also make sure the water in your bain-marie comes two-thirds up the sides of your moulds during the cooking time: direct heat will make the pâté curdle.*

WINE

Choose a light, fruity, dry red wine from the Loire, made with Cabernet Franc grapes, to accompany the pâté: the tannins will be softened by the mouth-filling smoothness of the pâté, and the fruit of the wine will nicely match the raisins.

CANDLE IN FLOWERPOT

You could use flowerpots with candles as table centrepieces. Glue a church candle into a 15cm flowerpot, then arrange holly and other items around (here artificial holly, and miniature terracotta pots; you could use tiny cones). Place ribbon around the top of the pot just underneath the holly, finishing off with a bow. Thinner candles can be fixed into oasis in the pot.

POACHED SALMON AND SHELLFISH WITH SOFTENED LEEKS, BOK CHOY AND FRESH PASTA

For 4 people

Planning ahead: The shellfish *May be prepared and put in a pan with the salmon, white wine and aromatics before the beginning of your meal.*
The leeks and bok choy *Can be cooked in advance and reheated. Once cooked, they should be cooled quickly in a bowl over ice.*
The pasta *May be blanched – which means virtually cooked – a day before, and reheated at the last minute.*

4 pieces of salmon fillet (pavé), approx. 150-180g, and about 2cm thick

24 cockles, washed

24 mussels, washed and bearded

salt and pepper

20g ginger, sliced into 4 lengthways

100ml white wine

2 sprigs rosemary

FOR THE VEGETABLE GARNISH AND PASTA:

4 large leeks, white part only, well washed, approx. 250g

2 heads bok choy

50g unsalted butter

200ml water

100g fresh pasta (farfalle would be excellent), blanched (see above) and refreshed

TO FINISH:

50ml walnut oil

a pinch of caster sugar

COOKING THE SALMON AND SHELLFISH

Take a large saucepan with a lid, and scatter the cockles and mussels across the bottom.

Season the salmon with salt and pepper. Top each piece with a slice of ginger. Place the salmon in a single layer across the top of the shellfish. Pour over the white wine and add the sprigs of rosemary.

Top with the lid, then cook over a fierce heat for approximately 5 minutes. All of the shellfish should have opened and the salmon will be three-quarters cooked. Turn off the heat and leave to rest in a warm place with the lid on for another 5 minutes.

PREPARING THE VEGETABLE GARNISH

Cut the leeks into thin slices. Discard any flaccid outer leaves of the bok choy and cut each into six lengthways. Put both into a deep saucepan with the butter, water and 1 teaspoon salt. Bring to the boil, then leave to boil rapidly until the leeks are soft, about 10 minutes. Season with pepper and set aside.

FINISHING AND SERVING

The best plates for this dish are large deep soup plates. Cover the bottom of these with the leeks, bok choy and shellfish. Top this with the pieces of salmon, still topped with the ginger, and keep warm.

Put the juices from the shellfish back on the heat and remove the rosemary. Add the pasta and bring back to the boil, then add the walnut oil, the sugar and some pepper, and boil once more. Pour the sauce and pasta around the salmon and serve.

VARIATIONS

Sea bass, turbot or brill would be lovely cooked this way.

Oysters and their juices could be added to the sauce at the last minute and just warmed through. If doing this, do not add any salt beforehand.

If you cannot find bok choy, spinach or rocket could be used.

Olive oil could replace walnut oil if you prefer.

RB'S NOTES

Raw shellfish *Check that they are all tightly closed. If not, give them a light tap, and if they do not close of their own accord discard them.*

Cooking the salmon *In this recipe it is cooked medium so that it retains its moisture and all its wonderful juices and flavour. Should you like it more cooked, alter the initial cooking time accordingly.*

WINE

The flavour of the salmon
and other shellfish
will make a good marriage
with an Alsatian wine,
preferably from a
Tokay-Pinot Gris.

CRANBERRY STICKY TOPPED STEAMED PUDDING

For 4 people

Planning ahead: The cranberry compote *Make it at least a day before to allow the berries to macerate.*
The entire pudding *May be made a day or two in advance. At the beginning of your meal, put in a warm steam bath
to reheat slowly so it is ready for dessert time. Alternatively, you could reheat on low in the microwave.*

WINE

The cranberry pudding
needs a rich rather
than a sweet wine.
Try a sweet red such
as a Mavrodaphne
of Patras (from Greece),
or a Californian Black
Muscat (made with
the red variety of
Muscat called Muscat
de Hambourg).

150g unsalted butter
150g caster sugar
3 eggs, size 3
240g plain flour
15g baking powder
finely grated zest of 2 lemons
2 tablespoons milk

FOR THE TOPPING AND GARNISH:

400g cranberries
300g caster sugar
150ml ruby port

TO SERVE:

*200ml whipping cream,
whipped to soft peaks with a
few drops of vanilla essence*

PREPARING THE TOPPING AND GARNISH

Bring the sugar and 100ml of the port to the boil, then boil for 1 minute. Add the cranberries, turn the heat to its lowest setting, and simmer for 1 hour. The cranberries will be soft, sweetened and the liquid syrupy.

Spoon half of the cranberries into four pudding moulds (basins of about 200ml volume). Add the 50ml of uncooked port to the remainder of the cranberries and refrigerate to use later as a garnish.

PREPARING AND COOKING THE PUDDING

Cream the butter and sugar together until a light straw colour. Beat the eggs together and pour into the butter mixture in a slow stream whilst still beating. Sift in the flour and baking powder, folding carefully in order to avoid forming lumps. Add the lemon zest and milk.

Spoon the mixture into the pudding basins over the top of the cranberries. Smooth the surface and cover with a round of greaseproof paper. Fasten a piece of foil with string over the top, leaving a little slack to allow for the pudding to expand.

Place inside a saucepan with a tight-fitting lid on top of a wire rack or a couple of folded cloths. Add water to come one-third up the height of the basins, and steam for 45 minutes. The water should boil during the full cooking time and remain a third of the way up the outside of the moulds. Top up if necessary.

Remove from the steamer, and allow to sit for a few minutes. If using immediately, turn out; if not, leave in the moulds until needed. A good test to see if they are ready is to insert a small knife in the centre; it should come out clean.

SERVING

Turn out the puddings and decorate with the reserved cranberry compote and perhaps a sprig of holly. Serve with the whipped cream on the side.

VARIATIONS

You can flavour the mixture with mandarin or orange instead of lemon. A vanilla custard would be excellent served with the pudding.

RB'S NOTES

Planning ahead *If reheating the puddings, leave them in the moulds until needed so that they do not get damaged.*

The pudding batter *Do not be tempted to add more milk, as it should be of a dropping consistency. If you add too much milk, the puddings will rise too much during the cooking and fall in the centre afterwards.*

MENU 3

If the idea of a roast at Christmas time is a little daunting or you just feel like something more wholesome, this menu is perfect. The scallops offer a light palette-awakening entrance to your meal. Then the rich combination of game meats mingles wonderfully underneath the pastry to produce an aroma once the pie is cut into that is literally heady. Perhaps take a little break and walk around the Christmas tree before the dessert of baked apples.

ESCABECHE OF SCALLOPS
WITH OLIVES, FENNEL AND
CORIANDER

RAYMOND BLANC'S GAME PIE

BAKED APPLES WITH
PISTACHIO CARAMEL AND
DRIED FRUITS

ESCABECHE OF SCALLOPS WITH OLIVES, FENNEL AND CORIANDER

For 6 people

Planning ahead: The scallops *Must be prepared at least a day in advance.*
The fennel and olive mixture *May be prepared 2-3 hours in advance.*
The finished dish *May be assembled 2 hours in advance and kept in a cool place.*

9 medium fresh scallops,
plus roes if available

3 medium shallots, peeled
and finely sliced

2 medium carrots, peeled
and finely sliced

150ml orange juice

75ml lemon juice

1 small bunch fresh coriander,
chopped

FOR THE FENNEL AND

OLIVE GARNISH:

2 fennel bulbs, washed and
cut in fine strips

100ml extra virgin olive oil

juice of 1 lemon

18 small black olives in oil and
herbs, stoned and halved

salt and pepper

FOR THE CORIANDER

PURÉE:

20g fresh coriander, leaves
and stalks

juice of ½ lemon

50ml olive oil

MARINATING THE SCALLOPS

Cut the scallops in half. Slice the roes thinly. Lay them flat in a tray.

Blanch the shallot in boiling water for 2 minutes, then rinse under cold running water. Drain well, then add to the scallops along with the carrot.

Bring the orange and lemon juices to the boil and pour them over the top of the scallops. Sprinkle the chopped coriander over this, and leave to marinate for at least 12 hours, turning occasionally.

PREPARING THE FENNEL AND

OLIVE GARNISH

Mix the fennel with the olive oil, lemon juice and halved black olives.

Season with salt and pepper. Set aside.

MAKING THE CORIANDER PURÉE

Purée all of the ingredients together in a food processor, or pound in a mortar and pestle. Season to taste, and set aside.

SERVING

Make little piles of fennel and olive in the middle of six plates. Arrange the scallops, roes, shallot and carrot around. Spoon the scallop marinade over and drizzle a little coriander purée over everything.

VARIATIONS

The scallops could be replaced by red mullet or sardines, but both of these would need to be lightly pan-fried before being marinated.

Basil or parsley could replace the coriander, and celery the fennel.

RB'S NOTES

The scallops *This recipe will only work if you use the very freshest scallops.*

The olives *Their quality is very important. Make sure to buy some in oil and herbs rather than in brine.*

WINE

A white Rioja, a Crianza made in the old style, will be full bodied but with a crisp acidity to match the marinated scallops.

RAYMOND BLANC'S GAME PIE

Serves 8 people generously

Planning ahead: *The game Ask your butcher to prepare the game, and to remove the flesh from the bone.*
The game stew May be made 2-3 days in advance.
The pastry May be rolled out, left to rest for 30 minutes in the fridge, then frozen. The pastry may be put on
the top of the pie, glazed, and the pie put in the oven about 25 minutes before you serve your starter.

1 x 900g haunch of venison,
cut into 5cm cubes

1 x 750g pheasant, cut into
8 pieces

1 x 750g wild duck, cut into
8 pieces

100ml groundnut oil

2 heaped teaspoons tomato paste

50g plain flour

salt and pepper

1-2 tablespoons redcurrant jelly

FOR THE MARINADE:

1 bottle Cabernet Sauvignon

2 carrots, peeled and cut
into 2cm cubes

3 onions, peeled and cut
into 2cm cubes

3 celery sticks, peeled and cut
into 2cm cubes

15 juniper berries and 10 black
peppercorns, crushed and tied
together in a little cheesecloth bag

2 bay leaves

1 large sprig thyme

FOR THE PASTRY
TOPPING:

500g bought puff pastry

1 egg, size 3, beaten

MARINATING THE GAME

In a large deep pan, reduce the red wine for the marinade by half. Remove from the heat, and add the vegetables, herbs and spices. Give a good stir, then add the venison, pheasant and wild duck. Stir again, then leave to marinate for 24 hours, stirring approximately every 6 hours.

COOKING THE GAME

Preheat the oven to 120°C/250°F/Gas ½.

Strain the meats and vegetables through a colander into a saucepan, being sure to keep the wine as this will be the base for your sauce. Pat the venison, duck, pheasant and vegetables dry between two cloths, or on kitchen paper.

Heat a large cast-iron casserole with half the groundnut oil and fry half of the meats until dark brown. Lift the meats out of the casserole into a bowl. Drain the fat out of the casserole, and add a little water. Scrape the juices off the bottom of the casserole into the water, and pour over the first half of the meats. Wash the casserole. Repeat this process with the remaining oil and meats.

Now return the meats to the casserole with the vegetables. Add the tomato paste and stir for 1 minute, then add the flour and stir for a further minute. Pour over the red wine and a little water just to come to the level of the meats, and add the herbs and spices. Bring all of this to the boil, cover, then cook in the preheated oven for 2½-3 hours, stirring occasionally.

When cooked, the meat should be tender but moist. Season to taste with salt and pepper. Sweeten slightly with the redcurrant jelly. Remove the packet of spices and the herbs. Set aside to cool completely.

PREPARING THE PASTRY TOPPING

Roll the puff pastry into the shape of your dish, but it should be at least 5cm larger on each side. Once rolled, leave to rest for 30 minutes in the fridge.

FINISHING AND SERVING

Preheat the oven to 190°C/375°F/Gas 5.

Put the cooled stew into an attractive ovenproof serving dish. Brush the edges of the pastry with a little of the beaten egg, and place on top of the meat dish to cover. Press the pastry well on to the sides of the dish to ensure that no steam escapes. Brush the top well with the remaining beaten egg, and bake in the preheated oven for 40 minutes.

Serve with some Mashed Potatoes (see page 141).

VARIATIONS

Wild boar could be used in place of venison, hare in place of the birds. A simpler and easier way to prepare the dish would be to cook the pastry separately, then heat the stew and put the pastry on top.

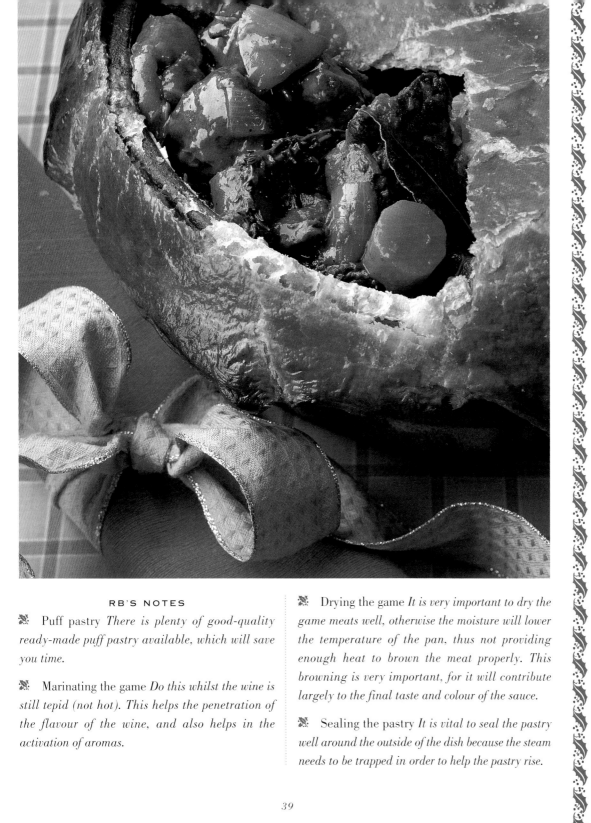

RB'S NOTES

⁂ Puff pastry *There is plenty of good-quality ready-made puff pastry available, which will save you time.*

⁂ Marinating the game *Do this whilst the wine is still tepid (not hot). This helps the penetration of the flavour of the wine, and also helps in the activation of aromas.*

⁂ Drying the game *It is very important to dry the game meats well, otherwise the moisture will lower the temperature of the pan, thus not providing enough heat to brown the meat properly. This browning is very important, for it will contribute largely to the final taste and colour of the sauce.*

⁂ Sealing the pastry *It is vital to seal the pastry well around the outside of the dish because the steam needs to be trapped in order to help the pastry rise.*

BAKED APPLES WITH PISTACHIO CARAMEL
AND DRIED FRUITS

For 6 people

Planning ahead: The stuffing and sauce *May be prepared 1 day in advance.*
The apples *Can be cooked earlier in the day and reheated.*

6 apples, approx. 250g each, peeled, cored and rubbed with the juice of ½ lemon

6 dried figs, finely chopped

90g dried apricots, finely chopped

75g raisins, finely chopped

30g dried breadcrumbs

150g butter

150ml whipping cream, whipped

FOR THE FIG GARNISH:

6 large dried figs, the very best quality available

300ml water

150g caster sugar

3 large cinnamon sticks, cut in half

FOR THE CARAMEL SAUCE:

250ml whipping cream

100g caster sugar

2 tablespoons water

25g shelled pistachio nuts

25g large raisins

Preheat the oven to 180°C/350°F/Gas 4.

STUFFING AND BAKING THE APPLES

Mix the figs, apricots, raisins, breadcrumbs and half the butter together. Fill the cavity of the apples with this mixture, pressing in as much as you can.

Place the apples on a small oven tray. Divide the remaining butter between them. Bake in the preheated oven for 35-45 minutes; they should be soft and puffing out.

MAKING THE FIG GARNISH

Mix the water, sugar and cinnamon in a pan. Bring to the boil and add the figs. Bring back to the boil and cool. Reserve.

MAKING THE CARAMEL SAUCE

Heat the cream to simmering point. In a separate, deep saucepan, cook the sugar and

water together gently until you have a dark caramel colour. Add half, then the rest of the cream, stir until incorporated, then add the pistachios and raisins. Reserve.

SERVING

Arrange an apple and a fig on each plate. Spoon some of the caramel sauce and a little of the whipped cream over each apple, making sure to top each one with a few bright green pistachios and fat raisins. Pierce each fig with a piece of cinnamon stick.

VARIATIONS

Vanilla or rum ice cream would be a nice addition.

RB'S NOTE

Apples *Make sure to use a variety of apple suited to baking, such as Bramleys (or Cox's Orange or Juna Gold).*

Making the caramel sauce *Be careful when adding the cream, for it will boil up on contact with the caramel. Add half at first, and stir it in well before adding the rest.*

NAPKINS

*Napkins can form an integral
part of the table arrangement.
Buy them to match, tone or
contrast with your tablecloth,
but you could easily make them.
You can fold them into intricate
shapes if you like, but they are
simplest when rolled and slotted
into a napkin ring. Or you could
tie them with an attractive
ribbon and bow.*

MENU 4

—

A menu composed of three classics, all slightly re-worked to their advantage. The cinnamon adds interest to and heightens the sweet richness of the pumpkin. The cream with the pork is set off by the slight bitterness of the chicory and rocket. The citrus salad acts as a foil to the richness of the crème caramel. However, this is not a menu for the light eater, this is Christmas at its escapist best. You have the rest of the year to eat healthily.

PUMPKIN AND CINNAMON
SOUP, CHEESE AND PUMPKIN
SEED CROÛTONS

FILLETS OF PORK IN PUFF
PASTRY, CEP CREAM,
CHICORY AND ROCKET

ORANGE CRÈME CARAMEL
WITH SALAD OF CITRUS
FRUITS

PUMPKIN AND CINNAMON SOUP, CHEESE AND PUMPKIN SEED CROÛTONS

For 6 people

Planning ahead: The soup and pumpkin shell *May be prepared in advance and reheated.*
The croûtons *May be toasted on one side and sprinkled with the cheese and pumpkin seeds, ready to finish at the last moment.*

1 ripe pumpkin, 3-4 kg in weight

50 ml grapeseed oil

1 large onion, peeled and finely chopped

salt and pepper

750 ml water

250 ml milk

2 cinnamon sticks, crushed and tied into a muslin bag

FOR THE CROÛTONS:

18 slices cut from a baguette, lightly buttered then toasted

75 g Gruyère cheese, finely grated

40 g pumpkin seeds, lightly toasted

3 egg yolks, size 3

Preheat the oven to 170°C/325-350°F/Gas 3-4.

PREPARING THE PUMPKIN

Slice the top off the pumpkin with your knife pointing inwards at an angle. Scoop out all of the seeds and discard them. Remove most of the flesh, taking care not to damage the shell. Set the lid and pumpkin shell aside.

MAKING THE SOUP

In a large saucepan, heat the grapeseed oil until it is at smoking point. Add the pumpkin flesh and the chopped onion. Toss over high heat for 3 minutes, then add 1 teaspoon salt and toss for a further minute.

Transfer to a deep saucepan, and cover with the water and milk. Add the cinnamon in the bag, then bring to the boil and cook at a rapid simmer for approximately 20 minutes. (The pumpkin should fall apart.) Remove the cinnamon bag, then liquidise, push through a sieve, and season to taste. Reserve.

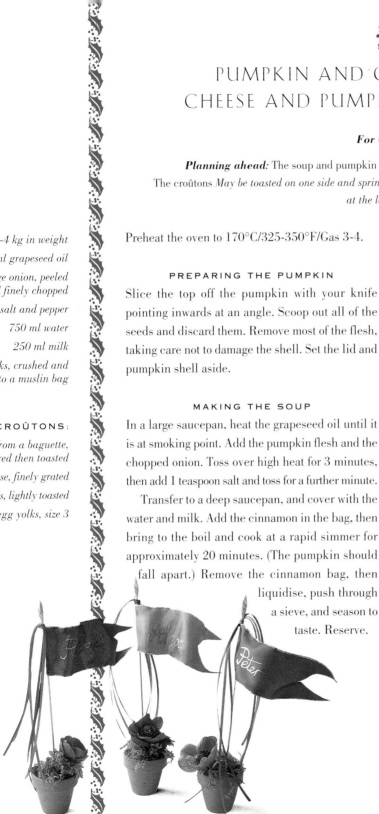

MAKING THE CROÛTONS

Mix the cheese with the pumpkin seeds and egg yolks. Season. Place a little mound of this mixture in the centre of each croûton, then place under the grill until lightly browned.

SERVING

Place the pumpkin tureen and lid separately on a tray in the preheated oven for approximately 30 minutes. Heat the soup and pour into the hot pumpkin. Top with the lid and serve to your guests, with the croûtons offered separately.

VARIATIONS

A little Kirsch could be added, and grated nutmeg or allspice could replace the cinnamon. If you can find them, it would be delightful to serve the soup individually in small pumpkins.

RB'S NOTES

Making the soup *When made with a ripe pumpkin, the soup will have a lovely taste with a light background of cinnamon.*

Preparing the pumpkin *When cutting out the lid of the pumpkin, it is very important to cut inwards at an angle. If you cut straight down, the lid will fall inside when the pumpkin is cooked.*

SMALL PENNANT PLACE NAMES

You will need wooden kebab sticks, and some clay which hardens without firing. Form the clay into little finials for one end of the kebab sticks. When set, spray sticks and finials with gold paint. Cut wired ribbon into 13cm lengths, and make a V shape at one end. Write guests' names on the ribbon with a gold marker pen, and glue the straight edge around the kebab stick, under the finial. Add a few narrow ribbon streamers if you like. Place the pennant in a small flowerpot containing oasis, and cover the oasis with moss and/or flowers. (Oasis is a florists' accessory which holds flowers firmly in a container. There are several types and shapes available; if using with fresh material, oasis needs to be soaked in water first, and should not be allowed to dry out.)

FILLETS OF PORK IN PUFF PASTRY, CEP CREAM, CHICORY AND ROCKET

For 6 people

Planning ahead: The puff pastry *May be rolled, refrigerated for 1 hour, then frozen for a week or so in advance.*
The mushroom mixture *May be made a day or two in advance.*
The chicory and cep cream *May be cooked 3-4 hours in advance, then reheated at the time of serving.*

2 x 500g packets of puff pastry
2 trimmed fillets of pork,
approx. 400g each
50ml groundnut oil
salt and pepper
1 egg, size 3, beaten

FOR THE MUSHROOM STUFFING:

4 shallots, peeled and finely diced
20g butter
2 tablespoons groundnut oil
400g button mushrooms
50g stale bread
1 small bunch parsley, picked,
washed and dried

FOR THE CHICORY:

12 small heads of chicory
juice of ½ lemon
2 tablespoons groundnut oil
30g butter

PREPARING THE PORK AND THE PASTRY

Roll the puff pastry into four rectangles just over 30cm long and 15cm wide. Place each piece between sheets of greaseproof paper and refrigerate for at least 1 hour.

Heat the groundnut oil in a large frying pan until it reaches smoking point. Season the pork fillets well and fry on both sides until golden brown, approximately 1 minute on each side. Transfer the fillets to kitchen paper and leave to cool.

COOKING THE MUSHROOM STUFFING

Meanwhile, cook the shallot without colouring in the butter until transparent, about 3 minutes, then set aside.

Heat the oil until very hot in a large pan, and fry the mushrooms quickly until golden brown. Lift out of the pan on to kitchen paper.

Put the stale bread into the food processor, and blend until fine. Add the parsley, again blend until fine, then add the mushrooms. Blend, using the pulse button until you obtain a chunky diced mixture. Remove from the processor bowl, and stir in the shallots. Season to taste and set aside to cool completely.

ASSEMBLING THE PORK IN THE PASTRY

Preheat the oven to 180°C/350°F/Gas 4.

Take two of the pastry sheets from the fridge, and brush them lightly all over with some of the beaten egg. Spread a quarter of the mushroom stuffing about the same width and length as the pork fillet along the centre of each. This done, top each with a pork fillet, then cover this with the rest of the mushroom stuffing. Now place the remaining two sheets of pastry on top to encase the pork. Press well to seal the edges, then cut off any excess (you can use this for decoration). Brush the top with the beaten egg.

Refrigerate for 15 minutes, then bake in the preheated oven for 30 minutes. Remove from the oven and keep warm.

COOKING THE CHICORY

Meanwhile, trim the chicory, discarding any browning leaves, then rub them with the lemon juice and season well.

Heat the groundnut oil in a medium ovenproof pan, add the chicory heads and fry for a minute on each side. Add the butter to the pan, then bake in the preheated oven, turning occasionally, for 30 minutes until they are golden and the cores are tender.

MAKING THE CEP CREAM

First check the ceps and their soaking water for any sign of dirt. If there is any, filter it out, but

FOR THE CEP CREAM:

*30g dried ceps, soaked in
400ml warm water for 1 hour*

200ml whipping cream

**FOR THE ROCKET
GARNISH:**

20g butter

200g rocket leaves

keep the water. Bring the ceps in their water to the boil, and reduce until the liquid is thick and syrupy. Add the cream, bring back to the boil, and set aside. Do not reduce, as this will give a bitter flavour. Season to taste.

·FINISHING AND SERVING

Melt the butter in a large pan, add the rocket and cook for 1 minute, just softening it.

Decorate a carving board with the rocket and the chicory. Place the two pork fillets in the centre and carve at the table. Offer the sauce on the side, and serve with Roasted Jerusalem Artichokes (see page 138).

RB'S NOTES

The puff pastry *It must be rested for at least 1 hour in the fridge before using or freezing. This allows the pastry to rest and stops shrinkage.*

Assembling the pork in pastry *When 'wrapping' the pork in the puff pastry, do it on the dish you are going to cook in, because the pastry softens as you work it, making the pork in pastry very hard to transfer.*

Finishing the dish *It can be prepared only a maximum of 30 minutes before cooking because the moisture from the mushroom mixture and the pork will make the pastry soggy.*

ORANGE CRÈME CARAMEL WITH SALAD OF CITRUS FRUITS

Makes 1 large cream or 6 small creams

Planning ahead: The crème caramel *Needs to be made a day in advance.*
The citrus salad *Can also be made a day in advance and refrigerated under clingfilm.*

500ml milk

grated zest of 2 oranges

100g caster sugar

3 eggs, size 3

2 egg yolks, size 3

FOR THE CARAMEL:

150g caster sugar

50ml water

juice of ½ orange

FOR THE CITRUS SALAD:

2 blood oranges, peeled and segmented

1 pink or red grapefruit, peeled and segmented

1 orange, peeled and segmented

200ml Beaumes de Venise or similar sweet wine

50g caster sugar

Preheat the oven to 140°C/275°F/Gas 1, and have your mould or moulds at the ready next to the stove. Use a 1 litre mould, or smaller ramekins of about 7.5cm in diameter.

PREPARING THE CARAMEL

Over a medium heat cook the sugar and water gently to a dark brown colour. Take the pan off the heat, tilting it away from yourself, and quickly but carefully pour in the orange juice (the caramel will spit). Pour the caramel directly into the mould(s), and leave to harden.

MAKING THE ORANGE CREAM

Bring the milk to the boil with the orange zest and sugar. Remove from the heat and leave to cool.

Mix together the eggs and yolks and pour in the cooled milk through a strainer. Whisk well to combine. Check if the caramel has hardened in the bottom of the mould(s) before pouring this milk mixture over the top. Place in a water bath (or bain-marie) containing enough warm water to reach three-quarters up the height of the mould(s).

Place into the preheated oven and cook on the bottom shelf, uncovered. The large mould will take 1½ hours. Check that it is ready by inserting a knife blade into the centre; it should come out clean. If necessary, cook for a further 15-20 minutes. The small moulds should be checked after 40 minutes.

When ready, remove from the oven and the water bath. Cool a little, then leave to cool completely in the fridge (the small moulds for a minimum of 3 hours, 6 for the large mould).

PREPARING THE CITRUS SALAD

Place the citrus segments in a bowl, and squeeze over them the juice from the fruit cores.

Reduce the wine quickly with the sugar until syrupy. Allow to cool, then pour over the citrus segments.

SERVING

To get the orange cream out of its mould, run a knife blade around the outside, between orange cream and side of mould. Place your serving plate over the top, flip both over and the orange cream should come out. If not, give it a very *gentle* shake. Once out of the mould, decorate with the citrus salad. Pour the syrup over the top.

VARIATIONS

The cream can be infused with just about anything, and the fruit changed accordingly – vanilla and poached pears, ginger and dried apricot compote, cinnamon and diced caramelised apples.

The caramel *It is very important that the caramel hardens in the mould(s) before the addition of the cream, as otherwise the cream and caramel will mix together.*

Cooking the crème caramel *It's essential to use a water bath: the cream will cook slowly, and will not* curdle *on contact with direct heat. If perfectly cooked, the cream will be a little wobbly in the centre. When it cools, it will have set sufficiently to turn out.*

Cleaning up *When you have unmoulded your cream, you will have some hard caramel stuck to the bottom of the mould(s). Simply boil the mould(s) in a pot of water for 5 minutes, and the caramel will melt.*

WINE

A sweet wine from the Loire such as a Vouvray, preferably from a good vintage such as 1989 or 1990, will have enough acidity to match the citrus fruits.

AFTERNOON TEA

---

*The days leading up to Christmas and the few
days afterwards are notorious for surprise callers.
So, even though afternoon tea is obviously not a priority,
it pays to have a little something in the larder,
and the kettle never far off the boil. A Christmas cake is
usually in order, and a traditional British cake,
dense with dried fruit, is delicious. Here, however, I have
chosen different cake ideas from different countries –
from Germany, England and France. All of them are
simple to make, and keep reasonably well, so are good
for both a planned afternoon tea and just in case...*

STOLLEN

Just as with our mince pies, everyone has a different (their own, the best or the true original) recipe for Stollen, a German Christmas cake. After much research (not to mention tasting), we have been given a recipe that uses baking powder instead of yeast. The simplicity of preparation appealed, as did the end result!

Makes 1 log

Planning ahead: *A bit like a Christmas pudding. Some people will not touch it before a week, some people leave it for up to 4 weeks to let the flavours mingle. So the Stollen may be prepared well in advance.*

250g plain flour

10g baking powder

110g vanilla sugar

1 pinch powdered cardamom

1 pinch freshly grated nutmeg

1 tablespoon dark rum

2 drops bitter almond essence

1 egg and 1 yolk, size 3

100g unsalted butter, cut into small pieces

125g quark

grated zest of 1 lemon

40g mixed peel

60g slivered almonds

125g sultanas, nice fat ones

100g marzipan, chopped in small pieces

FOR THE GLAZE:

50g unsalted butter, melted

100g icing sugar

PREPARING THE DOUGH

Preheat the oven to 170°C/325-350°F/Gas 3-4.

Sift the flour and baking powder into a bowl, then mix in the sugar and spices. Make a little well in the centre and pour

in the rum, the almond essence, the egg and the yolk. Mix all of this until it forms a thick paste.

Add the small pieces of butter and the quark. Knead well until it forms a smooth dough. Now carefully add the lemon zest, mixed peel, almonds, sultanas and chopped marzipan. Do not work the dough too hard or you will discolour it.

FORMING AND COOKING THE STOLLEN

Sprinkle a little extra flour on a work surface and roll the dough out to a rectangle about 25 x 20cm. Roll it into an oval log and place on an oven tray lined with baking paper. Bake in the preheated oven for 45 minutes. Check after 20 minutes and if the Stollen is colouring too quickly, protect it with some foil.

Remove from the oven and coat the Stollen lavishly with the melted butter and icing sugar. Leave to cool on a wire rack, then wrap well in foil and keep in a cool place until needed.

RB'S NOTE

Marzipan *If you are a great fan of marzipan you could up the quantity by 50 per cent and instead of cutting it into small pieces roll it with some icing sugar into a sausage shape and roll it up in the dough. This will give you a surprise filling once the Stollen is cooked.*

MINCE PIES

Makes about 30

Planning ahead: The mincemeat *May be made 1 month in advance.*
The pies May be made and frozen, then cooked when needed.
Or, once cooked, they will keep in an airtight tin for 5 days; just pass
them quickly through the oven to freshen the pastry before serving.

FOR THE MINCEMEAT:
150g Bramley apples, finely chopped
125g (16) black seedless grapes, finely chopped
125g currants, chopped
150g sultanas, chopped

40g mixed peel, chopped
30g dried cranberries
60g nibbed almonds
zest and juice of 1 orange and 1 grapefruit
250g muscovado sugar
10g Chinese five-spice powder
5g powdered cardamom
1/2 cinnamon stick, powdered
100ml dark rum

FOR THE SWEET SHORTCRUST PASTRY:
250g unsalted butter
125g icing sugar
2 egg yolks, size 3
500g plain flour

TO FINISH:
1 egg, size 3, beaten
icing sugar

PREPARING THE MINCEMEAT
Mix all the ingredients together, stir well and refrigerate until needed.

MAKING THE PASTRY
Mix together the butter and icing sugar until they are completely blended. Add the egg yolks and finally the flour. Knead until you have a smooth dough. Leave to rest for at least 1 hour before using.

MAKING THE MINCE PIES
Preheat the oven to 190°C/375°F/Gas 5.

Roll the pastry out to a little less than 5mm thick. Cut out 30 rounds just a little larger than your tartelette moulds, and 30 rounds with the pastry cutter two sizes down (or, for fun, as we have done, some star shapes). Line the tartelette moulds (or muffin tins) with the large rounds of puff pastry. Fill them with mincemeat to level with the sides. Now brush a little beaten egg around the edges of the smaller rounds (or the stars) and stick them on top of the mince pies. Brush with a little more beaten egg, and then bake in the preheated oven for 25 minutes until golden brown.

Transfer from the moulds to a wire rack and leave to cool. Sprinkle generously with icing sugar.

LA GALETTE DES ROIS

This Twelfth Night cake commemorates the three magi or kings.
The tradition is to place a small china king and queen in the middle
of the cake, the crowns made of silver (the queen) and gold (the king), or
a red and a green pea. The lucky ones who find the queen or king in
their helping are king and queen for a day.

For 8 people

2 x 200g square pieces of best bought puff pastry
(made with butter)
100g plain flour
1 egg, size 3, beaten

FOR THE FRANGIPANE CREAM:

100g unsalted butter, softened
100g icing sugar
100g ground almonds
4 eggs, size 3
finely grated zest of 2 lemons
2 teaspoons almond essence

Preheat the oven to 200°C/400°F/Gas 6.

ROLLING OUT THE PUFF PASTRY

Lightly dust the table with some of the flour to prevent the puff pastry from sticking.

Place one piece of puff pastry in front of you and sprinkle it with a little more of the flour. Roll into a circle about 30cm in diameter and 2mm thick. Dust a tray with yet more flour, place the circle of pastry on it and refrigerate for about 30 minutes, so that the pastry will lose its elasticity; this will also prevent it shrinking during cooking.

Repeat the same process for the second piece of pastry.

PREPARING THE FRANGIPANE CREAM

While the pastry is resting, prepare the frangipane cream. Place the softened butter in a bowl and add the icing sugar. Whisk it in very well. Add the ground almonds and whisk into the mixture thoroughly. Add the eggs one by one along with the lemon zest and almond essence, whisking the mixture well after each egg has been added. Reserve.

BUILDING THE *GALETTE DES ROIS*

Line a baking sheet with greaseproof paper and reserve. Using a plate 28cm in diameter, cut out two circles from each of the puff pastry rounds. Place one of the pastry circles on the lined baking sheet and brush all around the edge of the circle with egg wash. Pour the frangipane cream in the middle of the circle and spread it over about 1cm thick to form a concentric circle about 2cm away from the edge of the pastry.

Place the second pastry circle on top of the frangipane cream and, using your fingertips, press all around the edge of the circle to seal the pastry together. Using a small knife, press down with the blade to scallop and make a fluted edge to the pastry; this also strengthens the join between the two circles of pastry. Glaze the top of the pastry with egg wash and, using a small knife again, lightly score it to create an attractive design.

COOKING THE *GALETTE DES ROIS*

Place in the preheated oven for 15 minutes, then reduce the temperature to 180°C/350°F/Gas 4, and cook for another 15 minutes. Remove from the oven, allow to cool for 15 minutes, then serve to your guests.

RB'S NOTES

※ Glazing the pastry *Be careful not to put egg wash on the sides of the puff pastry. The egg wash will stick to the layers and will prevent the pastry from rising. Be careful, too, not to cut through the puff pastry when you score it.*

※ Glazing the cake *At the end of the cooking you could, if you wished, glaze the top of the galette des rois to get a better shine. When you take the galette des rois from the oven, dust the top with icing sugar and place under the grill for 30 seconds until the icing sugar has melted.*

CORK RING

Buy a wicker or cork bark ring frame. Collect together a variety of corks from wine and Champagne bottles (there is no shortage of these at Le Manoir, especially at Christmas!). Remove the metal tops from the Champagne corks. Use a glue gun to stick the corks on all over the frame, either randomly or in an attractive pattern. When dry, spray-paint with gold, silver or a colour (they're good left natural, too). Attach a ribbon bow at the foot and a loop of ribbon at the top if you want to hang the ring. Otherwise it can sit on a surface with candles in the middle.

This might seem to be the wrong way round, with a pithivier (albeit of crab) at the beginning, and a soup (of sweet, new rhubarb) at the end, but no, it's just another example of a Christmas away from the ordinary, with a luscious rib of roasted Aberdeen Angus beef in the middle.

PITHIVIERS OF CRAB
WITH CARROT EMULSION
AND CORIANDER

RIB OF BEEF WITH CELERIAC
AND HORSERADISH PURÉE,
CELERIAC CHIPS AND
RED WINE SHALLOT SAUCE

RHUBARB SOUP WITH
FROZEN TANGERINE MOUSSE

PITHIVIERS OF CRAB WITH CARROT EMULSION AND CORIANDER

For 6 people

Planning ahead: The pithiviers *May be made up to 2 weeks in advance, frozen and then cooked from frozen. The sauce May be made a day or two in advance.*

200g white crab meat,
squeezed dry

50g unsalted butter

2 shallots, peeled and
finely chopped

1 carrot, peeled, washed
and grated

30g white bread or
cracker crumbs

salt and pepper

FOR THE PITHIVIERS:

plain flour for dusting

500g bought puff pastry rolled
to 2 rectangles (40 x 30cm,
approx. 3mm thickness), then
chilled for 1 hour

1 whole egg and 1 egg yolk,
size 3, beaten together

6 teaspoons soured cream

FOR THE SAUCE:

60g carrot, peeled and grated

50ml water

100ml olive oil

juice of ½ lemon

TO GARNISH:

1 small bunch coriander,
leaves picked from the stalks
and shredded

PREPARING THE CRAB MIXTURE

In a medium frying pan, melt the butter, add the chopped shallot and grated carrot, and cook slowly without colouring for approximately 5 minutes. Add the crab and cook for a further minute.

Remove from the heat and add the breadcrumbs. Mix well and season to taste. Leave to cool before using.

ASSEMBLING THE PITHIVIERS

Lightly flour a work surface with extra flour. Place one of the rectangles of puff pastry on this and brush it all over with some of the beaten egg. Leave the other pastry rectangle in the fridge. Mark the puff pastry six times with the dull side of an 8.5cm diameter pastry cutter. This is just to make an impression to use as a guide.

Divide the crab mixture between these six circles, making sure that it does not go over the edges. With the back of a small spoon make six wells in the centre of the mounds of crab. Place a spoonful of the soured cream inside each of these.

Remove the second rectangle of puff pastry from the fridge. Place it over the first pastry rectangle, the crab and the soured

cream, and press around the edges of the six crab mounds. Seal the edges well, then cut the six pithiviers out using a 10cm pastry cutter. Check that the edges are well sealed, then place in the freezer for 20 minutes.

Remove the pithiviers from the freezer, and cut a small round out of the very centre over the top of the soured cream. Then with the blade of a sharp knife, make small incisions from this hole downwards, not cutting through the pastry, just scoring lightly to decorate. Brush them lightly with the remaining egg wash and freeze until needed.

MAKING THE SAUCE

Place the grated carrot and water in the bowl of a blender. Blend at medium speed, slowly adding the olive oil until all is incorporated. Add the lemon juice, pass through a sieve, and season to taste.

COOKING AND SERVING
THE PITHIVIERS

Preheat the oven to 180°C/350°F/Gas 4.

Place the pithiviers on a baking sheet, and bake in the preheated oven for 12-15 minutes until golden brown.

Remove from the oven and serve with the warmed carrot emulsion, garnished with the shredded coriander.

RB'S NOTE

❧ The pastry *This is rested in the fridge to allow it to relax and prevent shrinkage. Also, if the pastry is cold, it will not stick to the work surface.*

❧ *The sizes of the pastry cutters can be smaller, or indeed you could use cups, but there must always be at least 1.5cm difference between the large and smaller cutters.*

Name cards are a nice idea (see page 109 for an even more elaborate presentation!), and little night lights in glass jars are effective but not glaring. Use a bowl of hyacinths – bought or grown at home – and decorate it with baubles in the same colour on top of some green moss. Add a splendid bow if you like.

WINE

Try a medium bodied, delicate and aromatic white wine to complement the crab pithivier, such as a Chardonnay from South Africa (which tends to have less oak than the Australian or Californian wines).

RIB OF BEEF WITH CELERIAC AND HORSERADISH PURÉE, CELERIAC CHIPS AND RED WINE SHALLOT SAUCE

For 6 people

Planning ahead: The beef *Ask your butcher to chine the meat and give you the trimmings.*
The celeriac and horseradish purée *Make a day or two in advance.*
The shallots *Blanch, then marinate in the reduced wine 3-4 days in advance.*
The celeriac chips *Make 6 hours in advance.*

1 x 3-bone rib of Aberdeen Angus beef, 3-3.25kg in weight, bones chined (trimmings kept)

1 carrot, roughly chopped

1 onion, peeled and roughly chopped

salt and pepper

water

FOR THE RED WINE SHALLOT SAUCE:

20 medium shallots, peeled

1 bottle full-bodied red wine (i.e. Bulgarian Cabernet Sauvignon)

FOR THE CELERIAC AND HORSERADISH PURÉE:

2 medium heads celeriac, peeled, washed and roughly chopped

150ml whipping cream, plus 50ml when reheating

50g butter

20g fresh horseradish, grated, or 60g creamed horseradish

FOR THE CELERIAC CHIPS:

1 medium head celeriac, peeled and washed

1 litre groundnut oil

COOKING THE SHALLOTS

Cover the shallots with cold water, then bring to the boil. Simmer for approximately 20 minutes until tender. Strain off all the water, then cover with the red wine. Reduce this until syrupy and about two-thirds of its original volume. Set aside.

ROASTING THE BEEF

Preheat the oven to 170°C/325-350°F/Gas 3-4.

Scatter the chopped carrot and onion over the bottom of a roasting tray with the beef trimmings. Season the beef with salt and pepper. Rub this in well. Place the beef on top of the vegetables and beef trimmings. Put in the oven and cook for 30 minutes. Pour 600ml water into the pan and cook for a further 1½ hours. Remove from the oven, leave to stand for 5 minutes, then lift out of the roasting tray and wrap in foil. Allow to rest in a warm place for at least 30 minutes and up to 2-3 hours.

Add 200ml water to the roasting tray, scrape the caramelised juices in the bottom of the pan into the water to dissolve them, and pass this through a sieve into a saucepan. Discard the vegetables and trimmings. Skim off all the fat and add the shallot and red wine mixture. Boil and reduce if necessary. Season to taste and set aside.

MAKING THE CELERIAC AND HORSERADISH PURÉE

Cover the diced celeriac with water and add 1 teaspoon salt. Boil until very soft, then strain through a fine sieve. Press with the back of a spoon to extract as much liquid as possible.

Heat the cream and melt the butter. The ingredients are best combined whilst they are all still warm. Put the cream, butter and celeriac in a blender or food processor, and purée until completely smooth. Add the horseradish, then season to taste. Set aside.

MAKING THE CELERIAC CHIPS

Cut the celeriac into four lengthways, then slice along widthways as thinly as possible. Prepare a flat dish with some absorbent paper or a cloth.

Heat the groundnut oil to 160°C/320°F, then fry the chips in three batches until golden brown, about 4-5 minutes. Transfer them to absorbent paper to drain. Reserve in a warm dry place.

FINISHING AND SERVING

If you have made the celeriac purée in advance, heat it gently in a deep pan with the 50ml cream, stirring constantly. Heat the sauce and beef if

necessary. Warm a large serving dish, put the rib of beef in the centre, and decorate with the shallots from the sauce. Serve the sauce, purée and chips separately and carve the beef at the table.

VARIATIONS

Parsnips could be used instead of the celeriac, and although shallots are best, if you cannot find any, use baby onions instead.

RB'S NOTES

※ The beef *Order your rib of beef well in advance to ensure it is properly hung and of top quality. This recipe is for medium rare; for medium, add 25 minutes to the cooking time.*

※ The celeriac chips *It is important the oil is not too hot or it will burn the chips before they are cooked; if the oil temperature is too low, the oil will permeate the chips and make them greasy.*

RHUBARB SOUP WITH
FROZEN TANGERINE MOUSSE

For 6 people

Planning ahead: The soup *Can be made 2-3 days in advance.*
The tangerine mousse *Must be frozen at least a day in advance, and can be made up to a week beforehand.*

375g rhubarb, roughly diced

150g rhubarb, sliced at an
angle, 6cm long and 5mm thick

375g caster sugar

600ml water

1 vanilla pod, split lengthways

**FOR THE FROZEN
TANGERINE MOUSSE**

(FILLS 6 X 100ML MOULDS):

juice of 15 tangerines

grated zest of 6 tangerines

100g caster sugar

4 tablespoons water

6 egg yolks, size 3

225ml whipping cream, whipped

FOR THE GARNISH:

6 mint sprigs

MAKING THE SOUP

In a deep pan, boil the 375g rhubarb together with the sugar and water. Simmer for approximately 5 minutes until the rhubarb has dissolved, then pass the liquid through a fine sieve into a clean pan. Discard the rhubarb purée. Add the vanilla pod to the liquid, then return the pan to the heat, and bring back to the boil. Add the diamonds of rhubarb, bring back to the boil, and boil for 1 minute. Transfer to a bowl and cool completely. Refrigerate until needed. Leave the vanilla pod in until you serve.

PREPARING THE FROZEN
TANGERINE MOUSSE

Heat a large saucepan of water to simmering point.

In a separate small saucepan, boil the juice of the tangerines with half the zest until it reduces down to about 2 tablespoons. Stir frequently to

ensure that the juice does not caramelise. You should have a texture of marmalade.

In yet another small pan, bring the sugar and water to the boil together, then add to the reduced tangerine concentrate. Set aside, but keep hot.

Whisk the egg yolks in a round-bottomed bowl over the barely simmering water in the large saucepan until thick. (A good indicator of the desired thickness is when you can make ribbons with the mixture off the end of your whisk.)

Slowly pour the hot sugar, water and tangerine juice into the mixture while continuing to whisk. Remove from the heat and whisk over ice until cold (if you have one, this whole process can be done in a mixer).

Once cold, gently fold in the whipped cream. Spoon into 6 x 100ml moulds and freeze to set, at least 6 hours.

SERVING

Dip the bottoms of the moulds into very hot water, then turn them out into the middle of six soup plates. Sprinkle the tops with the remaining zest. Pour the soup and rhubarb diamonds around and decorate with a sprig of mint, or some of the vanilla pod from the soup cut into batons.

VARIATIONS

The frozen mousse could be made with lemon, lime or orange. Or, to save time, you could buy a quality ice cream, sorbet or frozen yoghurt to put in its place.

RB'S NOTE

The mousse *The egg yolk mixture must be beaten until thick and then whisked until cold otherwise it will separate. Be careful not to overcook it, or your mousse will taste of eggs. The egg yolks are whisked over hot water to partially cook them; the addition of hot sugar will complete the process.*

WINE

A glass of a sweet sparkling wine like Clairette de Die will have enough acidity to match with the fruit of the soup, but the fizz will enhance the flavours of both.

CHRISTMAS CRACKERS

It is always difficult to find the 'perfect' cracker off the shelf - the colours don't match your proposed colour scheme, or they don't look glamorous enough - but with a little bit of ingenuity and imagination, you can achieve many different effects. Buy basic crackers made from paper and card to suit your colour scheme, and then get cracking. Wrap bows of thin ribbon round the ends of crackers, and stick on small pieces of lace or net, sequins, fancy buttons, little fans, paper scraps etc. to make a decoration.

MENU 6

The salmon parcel may be a little tongue in cheek, but nonetheless is an excellent combination of flavours, and could serve perhaps as everyone's last Christmas present of the day. There is something faintly reminiscent of ancient Rome in the main course, which pleases me immensely. Christmas is after all a time of excess. So, pick up the quails and eat them with your fingers; the most succulent parts are those closest to the bone. A quick orgy to induce digestion, then on to the luscious dessert.

SURPRISE PACKET OF SALMON
WITH A WARMED
APPLE DRESSING

ROASTED QUAILS WITH
SPINACH, VINE LEAVES AND
SULTANAS

ALMOND AND CHESTNUT
MILLEFEUILLES

SURPRISE PACKET OF SALMON WITH A WARMED APPLE DRESSING

For 4 people

Planning ahead: The tartare and parcels *May be made 4-6 hours in advance.*
The dressing *May be made a day in advance.*

200g fresh salmon, cut
into 1cm dice

2 small shallots, peeled and
finely diced

4 sprigs dill, finely chopped

½ teaspoon Dijon mustard

salt and pepper

juice of ½ lime

FOR THE DRESSING:

juice and grated zest of 2 limes

70ml grapeseed oil

1 tablespoon Calvados (optional)

100g peeled apple, finely diced
(1 large Granny Smith)

100g English cucumber,
finely diced

4 sprigs dill, finely chopped

**FOR WRAPPING AND
TYING THE PARCELS:**

4 thin slices pre-sliced smoked
salmon, each approx.
12cm square

1 young leek, cut in half lengthways, washed and trimmed into
8 ribbons 25cm long,
blanched and refreshed

FOR THE GARNISH:

50g corn salad (mâche)

PREPARING THE SALMON TARTARE

Mix the diced salmon with the shallot, dill and mustard. Season with salt to taste, then pepper, and finally add the lime juice. Set aside.

MAKING THE DRESSING

Mix all the ingredients together, and season with salt and pepper to taste.

WRAPPING AND TYING THE PARCELS

Lay the four squares of smoked salmon flat with the shiny side down. Distribute the salmon tartare evenly between them in central square shapes. Fold the sides over the top concealing the tartare completely. Make four crosses with the ribbons of leek on your work surface. Place each salmon parcel with the overlapping flaps side down on top of one of these crosses. Tie up with the leek, then refrigerate.

SERVING

In the centre of four plates, place a little pile of corn salad. Top each pile with some of the dressing and one of the parcels. Warm the rest of the dressing lightly and spoon around the outside. Serve to your guests.

VARIATIONS

The parcels may be filled with soured cream,

boiled egg, capers and parsley, and served with a horseradish vinaigrette. You can also use the crab mixture on page 13, but replace the dill in the dressing with coriander.

RB'S NOTE

🌿 Planning ahead *Do not be tempted to make the tartare too far in advance, for the lime and salt will cook the salmon, drawing out a lot of the moisture, and resulting in a very dry texture and unclear flavours.*

FRESH GARLANDS

Garlands can be placed on a mantelpiece, on a windowsill, over a door, along the bannisters, along the centre of a table (or around its edges), or around a fireguard (so long as it is some distance from the flames). Buy some florists' wire and reel wire. Cut a length of reel wire to the length required and a bit over. Cut conifer foliage, fresh holly (plain and variegated, and some with berries) and laurel into approximately 20cm pieces, and bind them attractively on to the reel wire. You can add accessories as you wish – cones, cinnamon sticks, baubles, fruits etc – binding them in as you move along the garland. (For a garland placed near a fire, oranges stuck with cloves are particularly striking visually, and smell good too!) Artificial materials can be used as well as fresh, and don't forget to add in some colourful ribbon bows.

CHRISTMAS TABLE RING

Buy an oasis ring frame, here of 40cm in diameter, then soak it with water if using fresh materials. Place on a plate and arrange in it fresh flowers such as freesia, cream roses, mixed floral and leaf foliage and a surprise ingredient – small lilac and white turnips! Loosely intertwine with ribbon. Fill the centre of the frame with candles of mixed sizes and heights.

ROASTED QUAILS WITH SPINACH, VINE LEAVES AND SULTANAS

For 4 people

Planning ahead: *The rice May be cooked 1-2 days in advance.*
The vine leaf parcels May be made 1-2 days in advance. They can be reheated with the grapes before you start your meal, and kept warm under foil until you need them.
The quails May be cooked a couple of hours in advance up to the point where they go in the oven and finished for 3-5 minutes at the time of serving.
The sauce May be made and finished at the same time as you are sealing the quails.
The spinach May be cooked a few hours in advance and reheated.

8 quails
50ml light olive oil
salt and pepper

FOR THE PILAFF:

1 small onion, peeled and finely chopped
50ml olive oil
100g long-grain rice, washed
200ml water
100g best-quality sultanas
1 tablespoon caraway seeds

FOR THE VINE-LEAF PACKETS AND THE GRAPES:

12 vine leaves (they can be found brined in most delis), rinsed and dried
70ml olive oil
4 bunches grapes, approx. 8 grapes per bunch, washed

MAKING THE PILAFF

Preheat the oven to 160°C/325°F/Gas 3.

In a small ovenproof and heatproof pan, cook the onion slowly in the olive oil until transparent. Add the rice and cook without colouring for a further minute. Mix in the water, sultanas and caraway seeds, top with greaseproof paper and cook in the preheated oven for 20 minutes. Check that the rice is completely cooked, then season to taste. Set aside.

STUFFING AND COOKING THE VINE LEAVES

Increase the oven temperature to 180°C/350°F/Gas 4.

Heat a large frying pan with a third of the olive oil. Fry four of the vine leaves for 30 seconds on each side. Remove quickly from the pan and drain on absorbent paper. Set aside in a warm dry place.

Divide the cooked pilaff evenly between the eight remaining vine leaves, then roll into thick cigars or balls. Place on a tray with the grapes and sprinkle with the remaining olive oil. Bake in the preheated oven for approximately 10 minutes. Keep warm.

COOKING THE QUAILS AND MAKING THE SAUCE

Heat the olive oil to smoking point in a large frying pan. Season the quails, then fry for 2 minutes on each thigh, then 1 minute with the top of the breast facing downwards, then turn them on their backs and finish in the oven for 3-5 minutes. Remove the quails from the oven and the pan. Place them breast downwards on a flat dish.

To make the sauce, drain the fat from the pan, then pour in the brown chicken stock, scraping the bottom of the pan to dissolve the caramelised juices. Add the figs and leave to infuse for 5

minutes. The figs will plump up. Remove from the stock using a slotted spoon. Season the stock and set aside.

PREPARING THE CREAMED SPINACH

Place the spinach in a deep saucepan with the cream. Cook for 3-4 minutes until the spinach has wilted and the cream is reduced. Season to taste with salt, pepper and nutmeg.

SERVING

On a large warm oval dish form eight piles of spinach. Top each with a quail and arrange the vine-leaf parcels in the middle and the figs around. Top four of the quails with a fried vine leaf, the remaining quails with the grapes, and serve the warm stock-sauce separately in a sauce boat. Let your guests help themselves.

RB'S NOTES

❧ The vine-leaf parcels *These can be made in any shape, so long as they are of uniform size and hold the rice.*

❧ Resting the quails *They should rest with their breasts facing downwards so that all the juices from the birds run through the flesh, moistening it and adding flavour.*

WINE

For the quail, choose a soft, full bodied and fruity red wine such as a village appellation from the Côte de Nuits (Vosne-Romanée is the most delicate wine of this region), or an interesting alternative, a white Pineau des Charentes – this fortified wine will have lots of fruit and a medium dry finish to match the sultanas.

FOR THE SAUCE:

200ml Brown Chicken Stock (see page 76)

4 large dried figs

FOR THE CREAMED SPINACH:

300g spinach, washed and tough stalks removed

100ml whipping cream

freshly grated nutmeg

ALMOND AND CHESTNUT MILLEFEUILLES

For 4 people

Planning ahead: The almond tuiles *May be made a day in advance and kept in an airtight container.*
The chestnut cream *Can be finished a day or two in advance then kept well clingfilmed in the fridge.*
The apricot coulis, almonds and chopped apricots *May be made a day in advance.*

FOR THE ALMOND TUILES:

50g unsalted butter

50g caster sugar

2 tablespoons glucose or corn syrup

1 tablespoon milk

150g almonds, sliced

FOR THE CHESTNUT CREAM:

350g sweetened chestnut purée

2 tablespoons rum (optional)

150ml double cream

FOR THE APRICOT COULIS AND GARNISH:

100g semi-dried apricots

100ml water

2 tablespoons caster sugar

BAKING THE ALMOND TUILES

Preheat the oven to 180°C/ 350°F/Gas 4.

Melt the butter with the sugar and glucose, then mix in the milk and then the almonds.

Make twelve well-spaced, tablespoon-sized piles on a non-stick tray (you will probably need to do this in two batches). Flatten them out a little and then bake in the preheated oven for 10 minutes. (They will be about 7cm in diameter.)

Remove from the oven and leave for approximately 30 seconds before slipping them off with a palette knife. (If you want perfectly round shapes, cut them with a pastry cutter as soon as they come out from the oven, but this is not necessary as they look lovely with ragged edges.) Reserve in an airtight container until needed.

MAKING THE CHESTNUT CREAM

Whisk the chestnut purée with the rum and a third of the double cream until smooth. Whisk the remainder of the cream to soft peaks, then fold in.

MAKING THE APRICOT COULIS

In a small saucepan, bring the apricots, water and sugar to the boil. Leave to boil for 1 minute, then remove from the heat and allow to marinate for 1 hour.

Bring back to the boil, then remove three apricots, and cut these each into four for the garnish. Purée the remainder. Set aside.

COOKING THE CRÈME ANGLAISE

Mix together the egg yolks and sugar in a bowl. Boil the milk with the vanilla pod, then pour over the yolk and sugar mixture, whisking constantly. Return to the pan and stir over gentle heat to bind, until it is thick enough to coat the back of a wooden spoon. Strain immediately into a bowl, stir for a further minute, then cool and refrigerate.

PREPARING THE CANDIED ALMONDS

Grease a small tray with a little oil.

In a small saucepan, cook the sugar and water together until a caramel colour. Toss in the almonds, keeping them separate, and give them each a coating of the caramel. Transfer from the pan on to the oiled tray with a small fork. Set aside.

SERVING

Divide the two sauces between four large plates.

Sprinkle the almonds and chopped apricots on top, then in the centre build the millefeuille, starting with the chestnut cream, then a tuile, followed by chestnut cream etc., until you have four three-tier desserts.

RB'S NOTES

❧ The chestnut purée *If you can only find unsweetened chestnut purée, add soft brown or muscovado sugar to taste.*

❧ The tuiles *These must be cooked on a non-stick tray, and then left to harden slightly before being lifted off. You will be left with some extra almond tuile mixture, but bake this to make wonderful petits fours.*

CHRISTMAS RIBBON BOWS

Ribbons come in many different widths, designs, colours and textures, and they come into their own at Christmas time, particularly in streamers and ribbon bows. By using those different textures and colours, a simple bow can look classic, elegant or exotic. Choose

your theme and colours first, then buy the ribbon of the correct width for the decoration you have in mind. The greater the width of ribbon, the longer it needs to be to get a bow which looks in proportion. Wired ribbons are now available which, although more expensive, can be 'moulded' to the shape you desire, and will stay in that shape. Bows can be used to finish off Christmas present wrappings, to tie napkins, to make Christmas tree decorations, to wrap round flowerpots and bowls holding arrangements, to decorate the backs of chairs and table edges, to bring colour to garlands, door and wall rings, and Christmas card displays. Tie them as you would a shoe lace, and pull the two loops to shape by smoothing and squeezing the ribbon.

FOR THE CRÈME ANGLAISE:

2 egg yolks

1 tablespoon caster sugar

100ml milk

¼ vanilla pod, split in half lengthways, chopped finely, or 4 drops of the best vanilla essence

FOR THE CANDIED ALMONDS:

vegetable oil

50g caster sugar

1 tablespoon water

20 whole blanched almonds

WINE

The characteristics of a Malmsey Madeira will perfectly match the particular flavours of the chestnuts and almonds.

MENU 7

The singing flavours lie in the garnishes and accompaniments in this Christmas menu starring prawns and guinea fowl. The vegetables complement the prawns perfectly in taste and texture, the sweetness of the carrots, cape gooseberries and beetroot offset the aromatic acidity of the lime, and the quince, walnut cream and crisp pastry add the finishing touches to one of my own passions – roasted bananas.

SALAD OF MARINATED
PRAWNS, SPINACH AND
SOUSED VEGETABLES

GUINEA FOWL WITH
CARROTS, GOOSEBERRIES,
BEETROOT AND LIME

ROASTED BANANA, WALNUT
CREAM AND FILO PASTRY
WITH QUINCE COMPOTE

SALAD OF MARINATED PRAWNS, SPINACH AND SOUSED VEGETABLES

For 4 people

Planning ahead: Everything can be made at least a day in advance. You may also arrange the food on the plates, just leaving the Parmesan tuiles to add at the time of serving.

10 fresh tiger prawns, halved lengthways

1 teaspoon grapeseed oil

2 tablespoons vegetable pickling liquid (see below)

1 teaspoon poppy seeds

1 tablespoon sesame seeds

FOR THE PICKLING LIQUID:

500ml water

100ml white wine vinegar

15 coriander seeds, crushed

10 black peppercorns, crushed

1 tablespoon clear honey

FOR THE VEGETABLES:

1 medium courgette, trimmed

1 medium carrot, peeled

50g white of leek, washed

100g button mushrooms, washed and halved

PREPARING THE PICKLING LIQUID

Mix all the ingredients together in a medium saucepan and bring to the boil.

PREPARING AND COOKING THE VEGETABLES

Using a vegetable peeler, slice the courgette and carrot lengthways into ribbons and with a small knife cut the leek into ribbons.

Plunge the carrot and leek ribbons into the boiling pickling liquid, bring back to the boil, then cook for 1 minute before adding the mushrooms and courgette. Remove from the heat, cool, then store in the cooking liquor.

PREPARING THE VINAIGRETTE

Whisk together the measured pickling liquor and oils. Add the bacon and grated egg, and season with salt and pepper. Set aside.

COOKING THE PRAWNS

Heat the grapeseed oil in a medium frying pan until it reaches smoking point. Toss in the prawns and fry for 1 minute. Add the pickling liquor and the poppy and sesame seeds. Leave to cool, then store in the liquor.

PREPARING THE PARMESAN TUILES

On a non-stick tray, make four rounds of grated Parmesan, then place under a grill until lightly coloured. Remove with a palette knife. Do this quickly because as the cheese hardens it becomes quite brittle and will break easily. Place on absorbent paper. (If making in advance, store in a dry warm place.)

SERVING

Drain the pickled vegetables (the liquor may be kept and re-used), and arrange attractively around the outside of four large plates.

Mix the spinach with the vinaigrette and make four piles in the centre of the vegetables. Spoon the prawns and their liquor over the spinach, top with the Parmesan tuiles, and serve.

VARIATIONS

Almost any vegetable could be used for the pickle, just alter the cooking time as necessary. Sardines or scallops could be used in place of the prawns.

FOR THE SPINACH
AND VINAIGRETTE:

*100g spinach, preferably baby,
tough stalks removed, washed
and spun dry*

*2 tablespoons vegetable
pickling liquid (see left)*

*50ml groundnut oil and
20ml sesame oil*

*2 bacon rashers, cut into small
strips and fried for 1 minute*

*1 hard-boiled egg, peeled
and grated*

salt and pepper

FOR THE PARMESAN
TUILES:

30g Parmesan, freshly grated

WINE

Try a Sauvignon from
New Zealand
(Marlborough) with
the prawn salad: its
grassy fruit can match
the flavours.

GUINEA FOWL WITH CARROTS, GOOSEBERRIES, BEETROOT AND LIME

For 4 people

Planning ahead: Brown Chicken Stock *This recipe makes about three times as much as you will need. It may be made and frozen in little containers a month in advance, or made 4 days in advance and refrigerated. As you will see in the other recipes, it has many uses.*
The guinea fowl May be cooked up to 3 hours in advance and then reheated for approximately 5 minutes at the time of serving.
The beetroot sauce May be made, up to the point of adding the butter and lime, 2 days in advance.
The carrots, gooseberries and fried parsley May be cooked on the day of the meal and reheated at the time of serving.

2 x 900g-1kg oven-ready
guinea fowl

salt and pepper

50ml groundnut oil

25g unsalted butter

FOR THE BROWN CHICKEN STOCK:

1.5kg chicken wings or
carcasses, finely chopped

100ml groundnut oil

1 medium onion, peeled and
finely chopped

1 garlic clove, peeled
and crushed

100g mushrooms, wiped
and chopped

1 tablespoon tomato purée

6 black peppercorns, crushed

½ bay leaf

1 sprig thyme

approx. 900ml water

10g arrowroot or cornflour,
diluted in 50ml water

MAKING THE BROWN CHICKEN STOCK

Preheat the oven to 225°C/425°F/Gas 7.

In a large roasting pan, heat the oil until smoking, then over the strongest heat, brown the chicken wings or carcasses for 8-10 minutes, stirring occasionally with a wooden spoon. Add the chopped onion, garlic and mushrooms and cook for another 5 minutes until lightly coloured. Roast in the preheated oven for 20 minutes until the chicken wings and vegetables turn a rich brown. Spoon out the excess fat and discard.

Add the tomato purée, peppercorns, bay leaf and thyme and stir. Deglaze the pan with 200ml of the water, scraping up all the caramelised bits from the bottom of the pan. Transfer the bones and liquid to a saucepan, cover with the remaining water, and bring to the boil. Skim, then simmer for 20-30 minutes.

Strain the juices and skim off any fat. Whisk the diluted arrowroot or cornflour and water into the stock, and bring to the boil to lightly bind the stock. Cool, then refrigerate or freeze.

ROASTING THE GUINEA FOWL

Preheat the oven to 180°C/350°F/Gas 4. Season the guinea fowl with salt and pepper.

Heat the groundnut oil in a large frying pan until it reaches smoking point. Fry the birds for 2 minutes on each side, and 1 minute on each breast. Add the butter and roast in the oven for 25 minutes, turning after 12 minutes and basting continuously. Remove the guinea fowl from the pan and place breast downwards on a flat dish. Allow them to rest for at least 20 minutes.

MAKING THE BEETROOT SAUCE

Place the beetroot, water, vinegar, port and sugar into a deep saucepan. Bring to the boil and simmer until the beetroot are tender, about 15-20 minutes, then reduce the liquid with the beetroot to a syruplike consistency. Add the brown chicken stock and bring back to the boil. Set aside.

PREPARING THE GARNISH

Preheat the oven to 180°C/350°F/Gas 4.

Scatter the cape gooseberries on to a small oven tray or pan. Sprinkle with the sugar, cook in the oven for 5 minutes, then set aside.

Meanwhile, heat the groundnut oil in a large frying pan until it reaches smoking point. Toss in the flat-leaf parsley, away from yourself, being careful as the oil will spit on contact. Toss for approximately 30 seconds until crisp, then transfer to absorbent paper.

FINISHING AND SERVING
Reheat the guinea fowl and carrots if necessary. Finish the sauce by bringing back to the boil, stirring in the butter and seasoning with the lime juice and zest, salt and pepper.

Arrange the carrots, beetroot and parsley around the outside of a large dish. Place the guinea fowl in the middle and pour the beetroot sauce over the top.

RB'S NOTE
The guinea fowl *This must rest after roasting, breast downwards, to allow the juices to flow through and moisten the breast.*

FOR THE BEETROOT SAUCE:

20 baby beetroot, washed and peeled, or 4 medium beetroot, washed, peeled and quartered

400ml water

50ml red wine vinegar

50ml ruby port

30g caster sugar

200ml Brown Chicken Stock (see left)

50g butter

zest and juice of 2 limes

FOR THE GARNISH:

Carrots with Cumin (see page 139)

20 cape gooseberries, opened, twisting the shell above the fruit

1 tablespoon caster sugar

20ml groundnut oil

1 small bunch flat-leaf parsley, washed, dried and picked

WINE
For the guinea fowl, choose a young red Zinfandel; in Australia this grape develops a good spicy, minty and soft fruit which should contrast nicely with the lime in the sauce and the cumin in the carrots, as well as matching the sweetness of the beetroot (Brown Brothers or Cape Mentelle).

ROASTED BANANA, WALNUT CREAM AND
FILO PASTRY WITH QUINCE COMPOTE

For 4 people

Planning ahead: The bananas *May be roasted before you serve your starter, left in the pan and reheated
in their own juices.*
The cream *Will keep refrigerated for about 2 days if well clingfilmed.*
The filo *May be cooked and kept in a warm dry place for a day then reheated at the same time as the bananas.*

Preheat the oven to 180°C/350°F/Gas 4.

COOKING THE BANANAS
Peel the bananas and rub them with the seeds from
the vanilla pod.

In an ovenproof dish, melt the butter just until it
starts to bubble, then add the bananas and vanilla.
Roast in the preheated oven for 3 minutes on each
side. Remove and set aside.

PREPARING THE QUINCE COMPOTE
Boil the sugar, water and vanilla pod together. Add
the quince and simmer for 15 minutes. The quince
will turn a pinkish colour and become tender.
Leave to cool in the syrup. (You can re-use this
syrup.)

MAKING THE WALNUT CREAM
In a deep saucepan bring the 30g walnuts and the
milk to the boil together. Pour into the bowl of a
blender and purée until smooth.

Meanwhile whisk the egg yolks and sugar
together until you obtain a pale cream colour. Pour
the walnut milk mixture over this and whisk
together, then return the mixture to the pan and stir
over a medium heat to bind until it thickly coats
the back of your spoon. Strain through a fine sieve
into a bowl, cool over ice and set aside.

BAKING THE FILO PASTRY
Preheat the oven to 180°C/350°F/Gas 4.

Brush the sheets of filo pastry with the melted

4 bananas

½ vanilla pod, cut lengthways

25g unsalted butter

FOR THE QUINCE COMPOTE:

2 large quince, peeled, seeded and cut in 8

150g caster sugar

500ml water

½ vanilla pod

FOR THE WALNUT CREAM:

30g walnuts, plus 20g to garnish

200ml milk

4 egg yolks, size 3

2 tablespoons caster sugar

FOR THE FILO PASTRY:

4 large sheets filo pastry

50g butter, melted

50g caster sugar

---

butter, then sprinkle the sugar liberally over. Cut each sheet diagonally into two pieces, then shape each piece over the top of an upside-down ramekin on a baking tray to make a hat shape. Bake for 5 minutes in the preheated oven. Set aside in a warm dry place.

SERVING

Preheat the oven to about 110°C/225°F/Gas ½.

Put the filo, bananas and garnishing walnuts in the oven to warm through.

Meanwhile spoon the walnut cream over the bottom of four plates and make little piles with the drained cold quince on the top of each.

Remove the bananas, the walnuts and the filo pastry from the oven. Place the bananas opposite the quince, then top with the filo. Sprinkle the walnuts around. Serve immediately.

WINE

For the roasted banana, go to town and open a wonderful bottle of Sauternes (or a Monbazillac): both must be from a warm and sunny vintage.

MENU 8

Vegetarians, do not despair! Here are three courses which are satisfying, full of flavour and suitably celebratory for both the eye and the palate. Tofu is transformed by the additions of mango and a nut sauce, and indeed the menu could very well be plundered by everyone else, especially those who are passionate about chocolate.

LEEK TERRINE WITH
ASPARAGUS, MUSTARD AND
HAZELNUT DRESSING

TOFU AND MANGO
BROCHETTE WITH A CASHEW
SATAY SAUCE AND
MUSHROOMS IN FILO PARCELS

CHOCOLATE MOUSSE WITH
CHOCOLATE LEAVES AND
CHERRY SAUCE

LEEK TERRINE WITH ASPARAGUS, MUSTARD AND HAZELNUT DRESSING

For 4-5 people

Planning ahead: The terrine *Needs to be made and pressed at least 24 hours in advance.*
The dressing May be made up to 2 weeks in advance (making double or more of the recipe and
having some handy is a good idea).
The asparagus and quail's eggs May be cooked on the day of the dinner. Finally, the entire dish,
excepting the dressing, may be arranged on plates about 1 hour or so before your dinner party.
Splash with the dressing at the moment of serving.

WINE

A white Côtes de Provence with its dry, full bodied and clean taste will be a good match for the leek terrine; its flavour will be enhanced by the acidity of the dressing, and it will have enough body to leave a nice round and soft taste in the mouth.

25 medium leeks, with the two outer fibrous layers and just the very ends of green removed, well washed

salt and pepper

FOR THE MUSTARD AND HAZELNUT DRESSING:

1 tablespoon Dijon mustard
50ml white wine vinegar
75ml hazelnut oil
75ml groundnut oil

FOR THE GARNISH:

6 quail's eggs
18 asparagus stalks
1 small bunch chervil, leaves picked

MAKING THE DRESSING

In a bowl whisk the mustard and vinegar together. Add the oils, whilst continuing to whisk. Season to taste with salt and pepper. Set aside.

BUILDING THE TERRINE

Put a very large pan of water on to boil. In the meantime, line a terrine mould 25cm long x 9cm wide x 8cm deep, with two layers of clingfilm. Leave some overlapping.

When the water comes to the boil salt it well, then plunge in the leeks and cook until soft, about 10-12 minutes, at a rapid boil. Once cooked refresh the leeks in iced water so that they keep their colour. As soon as the leeks are cold transfer them from the iced water on to a cloth in one layer. Press them well to remove as much water as possible. Trim to the length of the terrine, then set aside.

Pass the dried leeks, five at a time, through the vinaigrette. Build the terrine by placing five facing one way, five facing the other, green to white, until all of the leeks are finished. Cover with the overlapping clingfilm and a piece of foil-wrapped cardboard cut to the size of the terrine. Then press evenly under a weight for 24 hours. Do not be surprised at how much water comes out during the pressing. This is what should be happening. Just pour off as it appears.

COOKING THE QUAIL'S EGGS

Bring a small pan of water to the boil, delicately place in the quail's eggs, bring back to the boil and cook for 3 minutes. Cool under running water, shell and set aside.

COOKING THE ASPARAGUS

Cook in boiling salted water until just a little more than al dente. Refresh in iced water, then set aside.

FINISHING AND SERVING

Ease the leek terrine gently out of the mould, using the clingfilm. Cut into triangular wedges with a very sharp knife, and arrange on individual plates. Then remove the clingfilm delicately. Decorate the plates with the asparagus tips, and cut the stalks in slices on the bias to sprinkle around the plate. Cut each quail's egg in half and use to decorate.

Finally, add the chervil to the vinaigrette and mix in thoroughly. Pour over and around the terrine. Serve.

PASTA RING

Buy a wicker or cork bark ring frame. Collect together different shapes of pasta – the most interesting are bows, tubes and shells. Arrange these attractively all over the frame, placing them on at different angles. Use a glue gun to do this. When you have finished and the glue has dried, spray with spray paint (gold, silver or a colour). Finish off with a nice bow at the bottom with matching or contrasting tails and, if you like, a little arrangement, here

using silk leaves and gold painted acorns. Attach a loop of ribbon at the back of the frame so that you can hang it, on a door, on the wall, or in a window. You can do the same thing with corks and nuts (see pages 55 and 123).

VARIATION

If you do not feel confident about making the terrine, you could just make a salad using all the same ingredients. Instead of pressing the cooked leeks in a terrine, you could serve them in an attractive pile on a plate with the vinaigrette.

RB'S NOTES

🔸 The terrine *This is pressed to push the layers of leek together. You can use just about anything as a weight so long as it weighs about 1kg, and is distributed evenly. This amount of leeks serves 4-5 people so it only fills half of the terrine. Do not worry.*

🔸 *Do not be tempted to press the terrine for less than 24 hours, as it will be impossible to cut.*

TOFU AND MANGO BROCHETTE WITH A CASHEW SATAY SAUCE AND MUSHROOMS IN FILO PARCELS

For 4 people

Planning ahead: The brochettes and filo parcels *May be prepared a day in advance. They can also both be cooked just before you serve the starter, kept in a warm place and passed quickly through the oven to reheat when needed. The satay sauce Can be made up to 2 days beforehand and reheated, just adding a little water.*

300g tofu, cut in 8 x 3cm pieces and marinated in 50ml soy sauce

salt and pepper

1 medium courgette, trimmed, halved, then cut into 3cm squares

4 baby bok choy

1 mango, stone removed, flesh cut into 3cm squares

8 water chestnuts

3 tablespoons sesame oil

FOR THE FILO PARCELS:

8 sheets filo pastry

50ml groundnut oil

250g mixed mushrooms (i.e. shiitake, button, pied bleu)

30g ground almonds

2 tablespoons sesame seeds

2 tablespoons poppy seeds

50g unsalted butter, melted

8 chives, blanched and refreshed

PREPARING THE BROCHETTES

Have ready four skewers. Bring a large pan of salted water to the boil. Blanch the courgette and bok choy in it for 30 seconds, refresh in iced water and drain on a cloth or kitchen paper. Shape the bok choy into small rolls and set aside with the other ingredients.

On each skewer impale a piece of bok choy followed by mango, tofu, courgette and water chestnut, then repeat in the same order. Refrigerate the brochettes until needed.

PREPARING THE FILO PARCELS

Heat the groundnut oil in a large frying pan until it reaches smoking point and toss in the mushrooms. Fry for 2 minutes, then drain on kitchen paper. Roughly chop them whilst they are still warm, then mix them in a bowl with the ground almonds and 1 tablespoon each of the sesame and poppy seeds. Season to taste with salt and pepper.

On a clean, very dry work surface lay out 4 x 2 sheets of the filo pastry. Brush these liberally with most of the melted butter and distribute the mushroom mixture in central piles between them. Now pull up the sides, making little purse shapes. Drizzle the remaining butter over the top and sprinkle with the remaining poppy and sesame seeds.

Wind the chives around the tops, as if tying the

purses together, and place on a tray greased with extra butter and sprinkled with extra ground almonds. Set aside.

MAKING THE CASHEW SATAY SAUCE

Reserve 12 of the cashew nuts for garnish, and put the remainder in a medium saucepan with the remaining sauce ingredients. Bring all of this to the boil, simmer for 10 minutes, then purée in a blender and pass through a fine sieve. You will have a fairly thick sauce; if too thick, just add a little water.

FINISHING AND SERVING

Preheat the oven to 180°C/350°F/Gas 4.

Bake the parcels in the preheated oven for 5 minutes until crisp and golden brown.

While these are cooking, heat the sesame oil in a large frying pan until it reaches smoking point and fry the brochettes for 2 minutes on each side. Keep warm.

Heat the sauce and divide between four plates. Arrange the parcels and brochettes attractively, sprinkle a little soy sauce over the top and garnish with the reserved cashews.

VARIATION

This dish is effectively a combination of two ideas, and thus each element – brochette or filo parcel – may be used as a dish in its own right.

RB'S NOTE

The filo parcels *The ground almonds give flavour to the parcels, as well as helping to dry out the mushroom mixture. Do not be tempted to omit the almonds or your parcels will be soggy.*

FOR THE CASHEW SATAY SAUCE:

100g cashew nuts

1 teaspoon caraway seeds, crushed

1 teaspoon coriander seeds, crushed

1 tablespoon soy sauce

1 tablespoon grated ginger

150ml water

150ml coconut milk

TO FINISH:

2 tablespoons soy sauce

CHOCOLATE MOUSSE WITH CHOCOLATE LEAVES AND CHERRY SAUCE

For 4 people

Planning ahead: The chocolate leaves *May be made a day in advance and kept in an airtight container.*
The chocolate mousse *May be made up to 2 days in advance and kept well covered in the fridge.*
The sauce and orange zest *May be made up to 2 days beforehand and kept refrigerated.*

120g best-quality dark cooking chocolate

5 egg whites, size 3

40g caster sugar

2 egg yolks, size 3

FOR THE CHOCOLATE LEAF MIXTURE:

50g unsalted butter, softened

50g icing sugar

50g plain flour

2 egg whites, size 3

25g cocoa powder

FOR THE CHERRY SAUCE AND THE ZESTS:

1 x 250-350g tin of cherries and their juices (approx. 100ml)

150ml ruby port

50g caster sugar

2 cloves

juice and zest of 1 orange, zest removed with a zester

½ teaspoon arrowroot dissolved in 2 tablespoons of the orange juice

MAKING THE CHOCOLATE LEAF MIXTURE

In a medium bowl mix the soft butter and icing sugar together until smooth. Add the flour and beat out any lumps with a whisk. Next add the egg whites and continue whisking. Finish with the cocoa powder and make sure the mixture is completely smooth. Leave to rest in a cool place (not refrigerated) for half an hour.

MAKING THE CHOCOLATE MOUSSE

Break the chocolate into small pieces and place them in a large bowl. Melt in a bain-marie of warm water, stirring from time to time.

Beat the egg whites until they form soft peaks, then add the caster sugar and continue to whisk until firmer peaks are formed.

Stir the egg yolks into the warm melted chocolate. Briskly whisk one-third of the egg white into the chocolate mixture, then fold in the remaining egg white gently. Spoon the chocolate mousse into a large serving bowl or four individual dishes, and refrigerate for at least 3 hours.

MAKING THE CHERRY SAUCE

Mix the port with the juice from the cherries, the sugar, cloves and remaining orange juice, and reduce by two-thirds. Add the cherries and bring back to the boil. Thicken with the cornflour dissolved in the orange juice, reboil and set aside to cool. Once cool, you will have a sauce the texture of a thick syrup.

COOKING THE CHOCOLATE LEAVES

Preheat the oven to 170°C/325-350°F/Gas 3-4.

Make a template for the leaves by cutting an 8cm holly leaf shape in a piece of plastic (i.e. an ice-cream lid), leaving a frame around the sides.

On a non-stick tray, spread a thin layer of the leaf mixture over the top of this template, then lift it off. You will be left with the leaf shape on the tray. Repeat this 20 times (allow for a few breakages). Bake in the preheated oven for 3 minutes. Lift from the tray whilst still hot, and cool on a wire rack. Reserve in an airtight container.

SERVING

Spoon some of the sauce and the cherries around four plates. Put 2 spoonfuls of chocolate mousse on each plate and top each of these with a baked leaf, then another spoonful of mousse and finish with one more leaf. Decorate with the orange zests (and perhaps some holly) and serve.

RB'S NOTES

Zesting the orange *If you do not own a zester,*

just peel the orange with a vegetable peeler. Remove all of the pith and cut into very fine strips.

❧ The mousse *The egg whites must not be too stiff, as it would be difficult to incorporate them into the chocolate. The chocolate mousse would be too firm as well.*

❧ *The addition of only one-third of the egg white to the chocolate is to lighten the base; this then makes it easier to incorporate the remaining egg white.*

❧ The chocolate leaves *Make sure the leaves are kept in an airtight tin, otherwise they will lose all their crunch.*

Cut the centre out of a Savoy cabbage, approximately 10cm square. Fill this hole with some oasis, then arrange in this some ginger flowers and red roses; the

leaves of the cabbage look like exotic green foliage at the foot of the arrangement. Place a plate under the cabbage as it may leak water.

WINE

It's always difficult to match chocolate. Try a Rivesaltes rouge or a Banyuls (but not Rancio); the richness of such fortified wines will match the strong taste of the chocolate, and their sweetness the cherries.

PETITS FOURS

—

You have indulged, and have had a glorious evening.
Everyone has been brought up to date with the family
anecdotes, and of course you could not eat another
thing. But again here I am determined to further
sweeten your spirit via your tongue. You do not have to
make them all, just one or two. The kumquats on
page 133 make a lovely petit four as well. Wind down
afterwards in front of the fire with my wonderful
blackcurrant liqueur (see page 134), finish your wine,
or have a cup of coffee.

CALVADOS TRUFFLES

Makes 25 pieces

Planning ahead: *Make them a few days in advance, and keep chilled.*

90g extra bitter chocolate, flaked
50ml whipping cream
30ml Calvados
125g unsweetened cocoa powder
250g plain cooking chocolate, flaked, for the coating

MAKING THE FILLING

Place the bitter chocolate flakes in a bowl. Bring the whipping cream to the boil and pour it over the chocolate flakes. Whisk well to amalgamate, and melt the chocolate. Cool to room temperature.

Once the mixture has cooled, add the Calvados while whisking constantly. Continue whisking until the mixture has doubled in volume and is smooth in texture.

Now spoon the mixture into a piping bag with a 1cm diameter nozzle and as quickly as possible pipe into balls of 2cm diameter on to a tray lined with baking paper.

COATING THE TRUFFLES

Place the cocoa powder in a deep tray. Melt the flakes of chocolate in a bowl over a pan of warm water, stir well, and leave until the chocolate is just lukewarm.

Now, using a fork, dip the chocolate balls into the melted chocolate, then immediately place them in the cocoa powder and roll to coat. Place the truffles in a sieve and shake off the excess cocoa powder. Keep refrigerated until needed.

VARIATION

A glorious variation is to add some finely chopped marrons glacés to the mixture and exchange the Calvados for a well aged rum.

RB'S NOTE

 The coating chocolate is left to cool slightly so that the filling does not melt during this process.

DRIED FRUIT FIGS

Makes 15 pieces

Planning ahead: *May be made up to 2 days in advance and sugared just before serving.*

100g dried figs
100g dried apricots
50g granulated sugar

Chop the dried figs and apricots finely. Mix them together well, then make 15 balls, pressing so that they compact together. Pull up the tops to make the shapes of figs. Coat them in the granulated sugar and serve, in little paper cases.

PISTACHIO PRALINES
WITH DRIED PEARS

Makes 20 pieces

Planning ahead: *The pistachio clusters may be made a few days in advance and kept in an airtight container.*

150g pistachio nuts, shelled, blanched and peeled
150g icing sugar
100ml Poire William liqueur
20g unsalted butter
20 slices dried pear
20 uncooked pistachios, to garnish

MAKING THE PRALINE

Lightly oil a tray with a non-scented oil (groundnut).

Combine the pistachios, icing sugar and Poire William in a heavy bottomed saucepan and cook on a strong heat until the liqueur has evaporated and the sugar has a sandy texture. Reduce the heat and cook for a further 5 minutes, stirring continuously until lightly caramelised, then draw off the heat and stir in the butter. With a spoon separate the caramelised pistachios into around 20 little clusters. Leave to cool on the oiled tray.

If preparing them in advance store clusters at this stage in an airtight container.

FINISHING AND SERVING

With a pastry cutter cut rounds of the dried pears just slightly bigger than the clusters of pistachios, press the clusters into these, top with a bright green pistachio and serve.

HAZELNUT FINANCIERS

Makes 35 tartelettes, 3cm in diameter, 1cm deep

Planning ahead: *These may be cooked on the day and warmed through at the time of serving.*

60g unsalted butter
60g icing sugar
30g unpeeled ground hazelnuts
40g plain flour
1 teaspoon self-raising flour
75g (2) egg whites
butter for greasing
35 whole roasted hazelnuts

Preheat the oven to 200°C/400°F/Gas 6.

Cook the butter in a small saucepan over a low heat until it is lightly browned and scented of hazelnuts. Pass through a very fine sieve into a bowl. Set aside, keep warm.

Mix together the icing sugar, ground hazelnuts and flours. Pour in the egg whites and mix with a wooden spoon until smooth. Gradually mix in the warm butter.

Butter the tartelette moulds and fill them to the brim with the mixture. Plant a whole hazelnut in the middle of each, and bake in the preheated oven for 5 minutes. Remove from the moulds while they are still hot.

RB'S NOTE

These financiers are best served warm so pass them quickly through a medium oven before serving.

SESAME AND POPPY SEED TUILES

Makes 16 pieces

Planning ahead: *May be made 2 days in advance and stored in an airtight container.*

100g sesame seeds
30g poppy seeds
150g icing sugar
50g plain flour
35ml orange juice
100g unsalted butter, melted

Preheat the oven to 160°C/325°F/Gas 3.

Mix together all of the dry ingredients in a bowl. Add the orange juice and butter, and mix until smooth. Using all of the mixture, put 16 spoonfuls on a large non-stick tray (or use two trays). Refrigerate for an hour.

Flatten the mixture to discs about 5cm in diameter, and as thin as possible, using the base of a small flat-bottomed bowl. Dip this in very hot water each time before using so that the mixture does not stick. Bake in the preheated oven for 6-8 minutes until golden brown.

Remove from the oven and allow to rest for 30 seconds (but not to harden). Remove them from the tray with a palette knife and shape them over a rolling pin or wine bottle (you have probably just finished one, it is Christmas, after all). Leave to harden, then very delicately store in an airtight container.

SWEET THINGS

Bought sweets wrapped in cellophane are interesting visually, but why not try wrapping your own – the kumquats or the truffles on pages 133 or 90 could be wrapped in little pieces of colourful cellophane and scattered around the table. Twist to close, or tie with lengths of thin ribbon. These remind me of the papillotes *of my childhood.*

MENU 9

*A traditional French Christmas meal, chez Blanc,
with my sons Olivier and Sebastien. Personally I adore
all that comes from the sea, either raw or cooked.
All I saw when I was young growing up in Besançon was
the odd trout, so I make up for it now! Although
goose is traditional in France, I have anglicised the
cooking and presentation a little - but then I have been
here for so long I cannot help but develop a taste
for some things English.*

PLATEAU DE FRUITS DE MER

ROASTED GOOSE WITH
CHESTNUTS

BÛCHE DE NOËL AUX
MARRONS GLACÉS, SAUCE
AU CHOCOLAT

PLATEAU DE FRUITS DE MER

It is all a question of taste: some people have a passion for seafood, and some detest it.
I have only one rule – all seafood raw or cooked must be fresh, fresh, fresh!

Serve with a little mayonnaise, some chopped shallots in half white wine and half white wine vinegar, plenty of fresh lemons, quality crusty bread and good unsalted butter.

YOUR PLATEAU
COULD INCLUDE SOME
OR ALL OF THE
FOLLOWING:

Mussels just opened in a little white wine

Cockles and whelks

Oysters, freshly opened

Lobsters, simply boiled (see page 124)

Langoustines, simply boiled

Crabs, simply boiled

Tiger prawns, simply boiled

Sea urchins

A MARINE THEME

Shells come in all shapes, sizes and colours, some shimmering with mother of pearl, some encrusted with barnacles or coral. They can be used decoratively at Christmas, on the table as here, or on other surfaces, along with baubles, leaves, pieces of foliage, ribbons and crackers. They also look good arranged around the platter holding a tureen of shellfish chowder on page 115.

ROASTED GOOSE WITH CHESTNUTS

Serve with vegetables such as roasted parsnips, carrots and Jerusalem artichokes,
and Braised Red Cabbage (see page 137).

For 10 people

Planning ahead: The goose *May* be cooked before the meal, then left to rest in the foil
in a warm place, while the sauce is being made.
The stuffing Can be made the day before.

1 x 5.5kg oven-ready goose,
neck chopped for a trivet

salt and pepper

FOR THE STUFFING:

1kg rough sausagemeat

30g butter

1 large onion, peeled and
finely chopped

10 juniper berries

200g chestnuts (peeled weight),
roughly chopped

2 eggs, size 3

1 small bunch fresh sage,
finely chopped

100g breadcrumbs

ground allspice

FOR THE SAUCE:

chopped neck of the goose

300ml Brown Chicken Stock
(see page 76)

100ml water

PREPARING THE STUFFING

In a medium saucepan melt the butter, then add the chopped onion and juniper berries. Cook without colouring for 5 minutes until soft. Leave to cool.

Once the onion has cooled, remove the juniper berries and discard. Mix the onion with the rest of the ingredients for the stuffing. Season well with salt, pepper and allspice, and set aside.

ROASTING THE GOOSE AND MAKING THE SAUCE

Preheat the oven to 220°C/425°F/Gas 7.

With the blade of a sharp knife or a pair of tweezers, remove all of the feather stubs from the goose. Then with the very tip of the knife point score very light criss-cross lines across the breast and legs (this will look attractive and ensure that the fat runs out easily).

Now lift up the neck flap of the goose and push as much stuffing as will go into it. Fold the flap back over and either truss it down or secure it with a skewer. Turn the bird and push the remaining stuffing into the body cavity. Season well with salt and pepper, then place on a wire rack and the chopped neck in an oven tray. Roast in the preheated oven for 30 minutes. Drain off the fat, then turn the oven down to 180°C/350°F/Gas 4 and roast for a further 2 hours. To test for doneness, pierce the thigh. If the juices run clear, your goose is cooked!

Remove from the oven and wrap in foil. Allow to rest for at least 30 minutes. Drain the fat from the roasting tray, then pour the brown chicken stock and water into the tray. Scrape off all the caramelised juices on the bottom of the tray. Bring to the boil and simmer for 5 minutes, then strain through a sieve into a clean saucepan. Set aside.

SERVING

Heat a large dish, put the goose in the middle, and arrange your vegetables around. Serve the sauce as you carve at the table.

SHELL ARRANGEMENT

If you have a large shell, it can be used as the basis for a marine side table arrangement as here. Place some oasis in the shell, then place some spiky pieces of Christmas foliage (artificial or fresh), at the back. Place some iris in next, grouping them at the base of the shell, then arrange other smaller shells all around in the shell and on the table, as if spilling out of the large shell. Some pieces of real fan coral look lovely pushed into the oasis as well.

WINE

For the goose, try a splendid claret, or a Madiran or Cahors with a good tannic structure and a bit of age.

BÛCHE DE NOËL AUX MARRONS GLACÉS, SAUCE AU CHOCOLAT

For 10 people

Planning ahead: The bûche parfait *Can be made and frozen up to a week before.*
The chocolate sauce *May be made up to 2 days in advance.*

120g chestnuts in syrup
(marrons glacés)

3 tablespoons dark rum

200g sweetened chestnut purée

200g unsweetened
chestnut purée

200ml whipping cream

FOR THE SABAYON:

7 egg yolks, size 3

165ml chestnut syrup (from the
marrons glacés), or make a
syrup with 100g caster sugar
plus 65ml water

**FOR COVERING THE
PARFAIT:**

150ml whipping cream

30g caster sugar

chocolate flakes to decorate

**FOR THE CHOCOLATE
SAUCE:**

100g good dark chocolate

200g caster sugar

400ml water

70g cocoa powder

PREPARING THE MARRONS GLACÉS AND THE CHESTNUT PURÉE

Drain the marrons glacés and keep the syrup. Break the marrons glacés into pieces, place in a bowl together with 1 tablespoon of the rum, and leave to marinate.

Liquidise the two chestnut purées together with the remaining rum. Reserve.

MAKING THE SABAYON

Mix the egg yolks together in an electric mixer at high speed for 6-7 minutes, or until the yolks have tripled in volume.

Separately boil the chestnut syrup to 120°C/ 248°F. When the syrup is ready lower the speed of the mixer and trickle the boiling syrup on to the egg yolks, pouring between the sides of the bowl and the beaters. Mix well, then leave to cool.

ASSEMBLING THE PARFAIT

Whip the cream. Mix together the chestnut purée and the marrons glacés, then add the whipped cream. Mix lightly, then fold in the sabayon with a spatula.

Line a terrine mould (28cm long x 8cm wide x 7cm deep) with greaseproof paper. Pour in the parfait mixture and smooth the top with a palette knife. Place in the freezer for a minimum of 6 hours.

COVERING THE PARFAIT

Place a flat serving plate in the freezer.

Dip the terrine mould in hot water to loosen the sides of the parfait, then ease the parfait out on to the chilled serving plate. Peel off the paper.

Whip the cream with the sugar to make a crème Chantilly. Fill a ridge-nozzled piping bag with cream and pipe over the parfait. Return to the freezer.

MAKING THE CHOCOLATE SAUCE

In a medium saucepan, slowly melt all of the ingredients together. Bring slowly to the boil, stirring well, then pass through a fine sieve and leave to cool.

SERVING

Serve the bûche on the serving plate surrounded by the chocolate sauce. Decorate with some chocolate flakes.

RB'S NOTES

❀ The mould *You can use a special mould with a rounded bottom, or a rectangular terrine. If the latter, you can round the top angles off before covering with Chantilly cream.*

❀ The bûche *You can garnish the bûche with some extra marrons glacés if you like.*

❀ Serving *The bûche needs to come out of the freezer about 10 minutes before serving, otherwise it will be extremely hard to slice.*

WINE

The Christmas log will be perfectly matched by a Champagne such as Veuve Clicquot but, on a cheaper scale, don't ever be afraid to try something like a Moscato d'Asti – a great deal of effort has been put into producing these wines to a high standard.

MENU 10

A splendid four-course menu, with a blend of tastes and textures, of western and eastern ingredients and flavours. It has at its heart some delicious Scottish salmon, followed by pheasant, thus the celebratory tartan trappings of the table.

CREAM OF CHESTNUT,
WILD MUSHROOM
AND PARSNIP SOUP WITH
PARSNIP CHIPS

CARPACCIO OF SALMON
WITH FRESH PARMESAN
SHAVINGS

ROASTED PHEASANT, PEAR
AND PUMPKIN WITH A PEAR
AND VANILLA PURÉE

COCONUT AND CARDAMOM
BAVAROIS, PINEAPPLE
AND LIME SYRUP

CREAM OF CHESTNUT, WILD MUSHROOM AND PARSNIP SOUP WITH PARSNIP CHIPS

For 4 people

Planning ahead: The soup *May be made a day in advance.*
The parsnip chips *Can be made early on the day of the lunch or dinner, then kept in a warm dry place.*

2 large parsnips, peeled, topped,
tailed and washed

50ml grapeseed oil

300g chestnuts, peeled
(see RB's Note)

150g button mushrooms,
washed and dried

10g dried ceps, soaked in 600ml
warm water for 1 hour

400ml milk

salt and pepper

100ml double cream

FOR THE PARSNIP CHIPS:

2 large parsnips, peeled, topped,
tailed and washed

500ml grapeseed oil

PREPARING THE SOUP

Chop the parsnips into rough dice.

Heat the grapeseed oil in a large frying pan until smoking. Add the chestnuts, button mushrooms and parsnip dice. Toss for 3-4 minutes until all are a light golden colour. Drain off the fat and place the vegetables in a large pan.

Check the ceps and their soaking water for any sign of dirt. If there is any, filter it out, but keep the water. Pass the liquid through a fine sieve over the top of the mushrooms, chestnuts and parsnips. Add the ceps and cover with the milk. Cook at a rapid simmer for 10 minutes. Liquidise and pass through a sieve, then season to taste. Reserve.

MAKING THE CHIPS

Using a vegetable peeler, cut the parsnips into long thin ribbons.

Heat the grapeseed oil in a heavy-bottomed pan over a medium heat until it reaches 160°C/320°F. Deep-fry the parsnip ribbons until they are golden brown in colour. Lift out with a slotted spoon on to absorbent paper.

SERVING

Heat the soup, adding a little more milk if it is too thick, and seasoning as necessary. Serve in warmed soup plates with a swirl of cream, and place a large bowl of parsnip chips on the table for all to help themselves.

RB'S NOTE

The chestnuts *For this recipe these are best prepared by roasting. Make an incision on the top of each chestnut and roast on a tray in a very hot oven for approximately 15 minutes. The shells should start to open. Peel whilst still warm. Count on finishing with about half of the original weight.*

TARTAN CHAIR DECORATIONS

Cut some heavy-duty curtain stiffening into rectangles of about 50 x 30cm, one per chair. Buy some material, preferably washable, about 115cm wide, and cut it into metre lengths for each chair. (This material should be used for the table cloth as well.) Cover the rectangle of stiffening with about half the metre length of material, folding it round as if tying a parcel, long sides into the middle first, then the short sides. Sew these ends of material together to form a rectangle shape, one side of which, the front, is stiffened. Using a heavy-duty sewing needle, use gathering stitches to sew through both sides of the rectangle in the middle to make a classic bow shape when you pull on the stitches. Secure.

Fold the rest of the material into a scarf shape and gather at the centre, then stitch down. Sew this sewn part to the back of the bow, and finish off by fraying the

hanging ends. Thread a metre of thin ribbon under the tails and bring to the top. Knot to form a firm fixing point with two long ends to tie the whole thing to the back of the chair.

Arrange a little bunch of heather, some pheasant feathers and gold holly leaves into a small holly ring, and fix to the front of the bow so that the feathers rise above the centre of the bow.

CARPACCIO OF SALMON
WITH FRESH PARMESAN SHAVINGS

*This starter takes its name from Italy but I think it is more Asian in style. It is light,
which makes it the perfect second starter for a menu such as this.*

For 4 people

Planning ahead: The salmon *Must be cured in advance. It may then be kept, clingfilmed and
refrigerated, for up to 3 days.*
The vinaigrette *May be made days or weeks before you need it (you could even make a little more
and have a dressing handy for a salad, a few tomatoes, whatever).*
The entire dish *May be plated 2-3 hours in advance. Sprinkle with the vinaigrette and slice the
mushrooms at the last moment.*

1 piece of salmon, weighing
400g, skin off and boneless

1½ tablespoons salt

1½ tablespoons sugar

1 teaspoon ground black pepper

20g fresh ginger, grated

1 bunch fresh coriander,
finely chopped

zest of ½ lemon, finely chopped

FOR THE VINAIGRETTE:

60ml virgin olive oil

20ml lemon juice

salt and pepper to taste

FOR THE GARNISH:

120g beansprouts

1 small or ½ large red onion,
peeled and finely chopped

20 pistachio nuts, shelled
and skinned

100g piece fresh Parmesan

4 large firm white button
mushrooms

MARINATING THE SALMON

Mix together the salt, sugar, pepper, grated ginger,
coriander and lemon zest. Place your piece of
salmon, the side where the skin would have been
facing downwards, on a flat dish. Cover with the
mixture and press in lightly. Wrap with clingfilm
and leave to marinate for 12-18 hours.

When the salmon has marinated for this length
of time, just wipe off the mixture, give the salmon
a very quick rinse, and pat dry. Set aside.

MAKING THE VINAIGRETTE

Mix the oil and lemon juice together, then season to
taste with salt and pepper.

FINISHING AND SERVING

Toss the beansprouts with half the red onion and a
little of the vinaigrette. Divide this between the
centres of four large plates.

Slice the salmon as thinly as possible and distribute over the beansprouts. Sprinkle the pistachios
and remaining red onion over the salmon. Using a
vegetable peeler, make long shavings of the
Parmesan which you then scatter around. Finish by
slicing the mushrooms finely over the top and dress
with the rest of the vinaigrette. Serve.

VARIATIONS

So long as the quantities of fish, salt, sugar and
pepper are respected, you can add any flavourings
you like to the marinade e.g. parsley or dill instead
of coriander, some lemongrass instead of ginger,
grated apple etc. The finished salmon may be served
with just some dressed salad, perhaps slightly
warmed on a bed of potatoes, or just as it is with
toast or grilled bread.

RB'S NOTE

Marinating the salmon *The length of time you
leave the salmon in its marinade depends on how
strongly you want your fish to be flavoured by it. Also
the longer you leave it the dryer it will become as the
salt serves to drain out the moisture, thus preserving
the salmon.*

WINE

If you have some
Chardonnay left from the
first course, you can
continue drinking it
with the salmon – or try
a lighter style of
Chardonnay from the
Mâconnais.

PHEASANT FEATHER ARRANGEMENT

To match the theme of the rest of the splendidly Scottish table, a basket was filled with water-soaked oasis, and in it were arranged pheasant feathers, gold holly leaves, red amaryllis, thistles, dried sea lavender and fresh foliage. The oasis should be in a dish or on a plate to prevent dripping.

ROASTED PHEASANT, PEAR AND PUMPKIN WITH A PEAR AND VANILLA PURÉE

For 4 people

Planning ahead: The pheasant, pears and pumpkin *May be cooked before the starter,*
left in a warm place and reheated.
The purée *May be made a day or two in advance.*
The lettuce parcels *May be made 1 day before.*

2 pheasants, weighing
800-900g each, oven-ready

50ml groundnut oil

20g butter

200g (peeled weight) pumpkin
(approx. ¼ pumpkin),
cut into small wedges

2 large pears, cored but not
peeled, each cut into six

salt and pepper

FOR THE SAUCE:

100ml water

200ml Brown Chicken Stock
(see page 76)

50g butter

**FOR THE PEAR AND
VANILLA PURÉE:**

2 large pears, approx. 500g
peeled weight, roughly chopped

juice of ½ lemon

30g butter

½ vanilla pod

**FOR THE LETTUCE
PARCELS:**

1 small iceberg lettuce

20g butter

freshly grated nutmeg

COOKING THE PHEASANT, PEARS AND PUMPKIN

Preheat the oven to 190°C/375°F/Gas 5.

Heat a large frying pan or roasting tray with the groundnut oil until it reaches smoking point. Add the pheasants, brown for 2 minutes on each thigh, then for 2 minutes on each breast. Add the butter, pumpkin and pears to the pan. Turn the pheasants on to their backs and place in the preheated oven. Roast for 30 minutes, turning everything after 15.

Remove the pheasants, pumpkin and pears from the pan. Place the pheasants, breasts down, on a flat dish with the pumpkin and the pears in a warm place.

Pour the fat from the pan and add the water and brown chicken stock. Scrape the caramelised juices off the bottom of the pan, then transfer to a saucepan and boil to reduce by a third. Set aside until needed.

MAKING THE PEAR AND VANILLA PURÉE

In a medium saucepan, mix together the pears, lemon juice, butter and vanilla pod. Cook slowly until pears are soft, approximately 15 minutes. Remove vanilla pod but scrape out the seeds and add them to the mixture. Purée all in a food processor until smooth. Set aside.

MAKING THE LETTUCE PARCELS

Remove the large outside leaves of the lettuce and blanch them for 30 seconds in boiling salted water. Refresh in iced water, and lay flat on absorbent kitchen paper. Shred the heart of the lettuce finely.

Heat the butter in a medium frying pan. Fry the shredded lettuce for 2 minutes until soft. Season well with salt, pepper and nutmeg. Leave to cool and then fill the lettuce leaves with this mixture. Fold over into a parcel, joins down, and set aside.

SERVING

Heat the pheasants, pears, pumpkin and lettuce parcels together in a large dish in a medium oven. Whilst these are heating, warm through the pear purée and the sauce, finishing the sauce by whisking in the 50g butter.

Serve the pheasants, pumpkin and lettuce parcels together, and the sauce and the purée separately.

VARIATION

You could roast guinea fowl instead of the pheasant.

PLACE CARDS

Little photograph frames made from cardboard make

wonderful 'place cards'. Put a photograph of the guest inside on the front, and place on the table. The menu was printed inside the card, and a short poem (suitably personal) was written on the other side. This can help a party get off to a good start, and makes an unusual memento of a splendid meal and occasion.

WINE

The pheasant needs a rich, gamey, soft and fruity wine like a young Pinot Noir from the Côte de Nuits or one of the very good ones from Oregon.

COCONUT AND CARDAMOM BAVAROIS, PINEAPPLE AND LIME SYRUP

For 4 people

Planning ahead: The complete dish *May be prepared up to 2 days in advance. It also may be plated,*
except for the dried pineapple slice, and refrigerated a couple of hours before your dinner.

2½ *gelatine leaves*

65ml *milk*

65ml *coconut milk, unsweetened*

6 *cardamom pods, crushed*
and chopped

3 *egg yolks, size 3*

90g *caster sugar*

150ml *whipping cream, whipped*

**FOR THE SYRUP AND
PINEAPPLE:**

1 *small pineapple, peeled*
and sliced paper thin

75g *caster sugar*

50g *water*

pulp of 2 passionfruit

grated zest and juice of 2 limes

4 *turns of black pepper*

FOR THE GARNISH:

1 *small mango, peeled, stoned*
and thinly sliced

4 *sprigs mint, lemon balm*
or lemon verbena

MAKING THE BAVAROIS

Soak the gelatine leaves in water to soften them.

In a heavy-bottomed pan, bring the milks and the cardamom to the boil.

Beat the egg yolks and sugar together until a pale straw colour. Pour the milk mixture on to the egg and sugar mixture, whisking continuously, then return to the saucepan. Stir to bind the custard over medium heat until it thickens and coats the back of a wooden spoon. Strain immediately through a sieve into a clean bowl.

Squeeze the gelatine dry. Add to the hot mixture and stir until completely dissolved. Leave the mixture to cool down to room temperature (not so cold that it hardens).

Once cool, add a third of the whipped cream quickly, then fold in the remainder. Spoon swiftly into 4 x shallow 125-150ml moulds, and leave to set.

PREPARING THE PINEAPPLE, SYRUP AND DRIED PINEAPPLE

Preheat the oven to its lowest setting (approximately 80°C/176°F). Lay the sliced pineapple flat in a tray.

Bring the sugar, water and passionfruit pulp to the boil in a small pan. Boil for 30 seconds, then pour over the sliced pineapple. Once this has cooled add the lime juice, grated zest and pepper.

Remove 8 slices of the pineapple, place them on a non-stick tray, and bake in the preheated very low oven for 2-3 hours until dry and slightly golden.

SERVING

Divide the sliced marinated pineapple in flat even layers between four large plates. Dip the moulds into hot water, and unmould on to the middle of each.

Pour the lime-flavoured syrup around the bavarois and over the top of the pineapple. Decorate with the mango, dried pineapple and a sprig of your chosen herb. Serve.

VARIATIONS

A ball of an exotic fruit sorbet could be placed on top of the bavarois, and orange or lemon could be used instead of lime with equal success.

WINE

For the bavarois, choose
a fortified Muscat wine
such as a French Muscat
de Beaumes-de-Venise,
a Muscat de Lunel or
a Moscatel de Setúbal
from Portugal.

MENU 11

The four dishes here are not heavy in themselves, but you might be well advised to take a break between courses – pull some crackers, sing a few Christmas carols....
It's not a meal to be eaten quickly, but one in which every element need to be individually savoured, from the earthy blend of goat's cheese and shiitake mushrooms, through the shellfish chowder and the venison, to the pear and figs in their bath of spiced wine.

SHIITAKE MUSHROOMS
WITH GOAT S CHEESE,
HAZELNUTS AND ROCKET

SHELLFISH CHOWDER
WITH NUTMEG, GINGER AND
WATERCRESS

LOIN OF VENISON WITH
BRAISED CELERY, POTATO
GALETTE AND MORELS

PEARS AND FIGS IN SPICED
WINE WITH CINNAMON
CREAM

SHIITAKE MUSHROOMS WITH GOAT'S CHEESE, HAZELNUTS AND ROCKET

For 4 people

Planning ahead: *The mushrooms May be prepared a day in advance with the cheese, and just grilled at the last minute.*
The vinaigrette May be prepared 1 week in advance.
The salad May be washed and dried hours in advance.

12 large shiitake mushrooms,
5-6cm in diameter

salt and pepper

2 tablespoons hazelnut oil

12 slices, 1cm thick, of a goat's
cheese such as St Maure,
not too mature

FOR THE ROCKET AND VINAIGRETTE:

50g rocket, ends trimmed,
washed and spun dry

2 tablespoons white wine
vinegar

2 tablespoons hazelnut oil

5 tablespoons groundnut oil

caster sugar

50g toasted hazelnuts, halved

TO FINISH:

1 small bunch chives, snipped

PREPARING THE MUSHROOMS

Preheat the oven to 180°C/350°F/Gas 4.

Trim the stalks from the shiitakes, wash caps and pat dry. Place on a small tray, then season with salt, pepper and hazelnut oil. Place in the oven for 5 minutes, then remove. Top with the slices of goat's cheese and set aside.

MAKING THE VINAIGRETTE

Mix together the white wine vinegar and oils in a bowl. Season with salt, pepper and sugar to taste. Add the hazelnuts and stir. Set aside.

SERVING

Preheat the grill. Grill the shiitakes and goat's cheese for approximately 5 minutes until golden brown.

Mix the rocket with the hazelnuts and dressing. Place in piles on four plates, and top with the mushrooms and cheese. Sprinkle with chives and serve.

VARIATIONS

In season you could substitute the shiitakes with ceps and top them with some beautiful Parmesan instead of the goat's cheese.

WINE

The goat's cheese flavour will dominate here, so try a full bodied white wine from the Jura, something like an Arbois. The quiet rustic taste of this will also go extremely well with the mushrooms.

SHELLFISH CHOWDER WITH NUTMEG, GINGER AND WATERCRESS

For 4–6 people

Planning ahead: The soup *May be made completely in advance up to the final finishing and serving stage.*

SWEATING THE VEGETABLES

In a medium saucepan, melt the butter without colouring. Add all of the remaining ingredients, then cook on a medium heat for approximately 5 minutes until the vegetables are soft but not coloured. Set aside.

COOKING THE MOLLUSCS

Place the mussels and cockles, white wine and water in a deep saucepan, cover with a lid and cook at a fierce heat for 3-4 minutes until all of the shells have opened. Pass through a fine sieve keeping the liquid. Leave to cool and then remove the molluscs from their shells.

FINISHING AND SERVING

Pour the mussel and cockle liquid over the sweated vegetables in a large pan and bring to the boil. Add the prawns and scallops, and simmer for approximately 2 minutes. Add the cream, cooked mussels, cockles and seaweed.

Season to taste, and add the watercress. Serve either in individual bowls or in a tureen for all to help themselves.

VARIATIONS

Almost any shellfish could be used: shrimps, clams, sea urchin, etc. Some slivers of fish could replace the scallops.

A little coriander could be added as well as or in place of the watercress. Equally some chopped fresh chilli could be sweated with the vegetables, or more cayenne added at the end to provide a spicier soup.

RB'S NOTES

Sweating the vegetables *This serves to soften them whilst removing their acidity and bitterness.*

Cooking the molluscs *If the mussels and cockles do not open after cooking it is safest to discard them. Similarly, if they do not close when firmly tapped before cooking, they are probably dead and should be discarded.*

WINE

A good Mâconnais wine, such as a Pouilly-Fuissé, with its crispness and slightly ripe fruit, will go well with the shellfish chowder.

---

2 dozen small mussels, bearded and washed

2 dozen small cockles, bearded and washed

200ml white wine

200ml water

FOR THE AROMATIC VEGETABLES:

30g butter

1 medium carrot, cut into 1.5cm dice

2 large shallots, peeled and cut into 1.5cm dice

50g celery, cut into 1.5cm dice

50g mushrooms, cut into 1.5cm dice

2 cloves garlic, peeled and finely chopped

20g ginger, peeled and finely chopped

TO FINISH:

8 tiger prawns, each cut in 3

4 scallops, cut in 6

100ml whipping cream

10g arame seaweed, reconstituted in a little water and rinsed

salt, pepper, nutmeg, cayenne and lemon juice to taste

1 small bunch watercress, washed and picked

LOIN OF VENISON WITH BRAISED CELERY, POTATO GALETTE AND MORELS

For 4 people

Planning ahead: The venison *Ask your butcher to bone and trim it for you, and chop the bones; you will finish with 2 loins weighing about 600g in total. (Order the venison well in advance if you like it matured.) May be sealed before you serve your starter, and then cooked in the preheated oven for 6 minutes when needed.*
The sauce *May be made a day or two in advance.*
The potato and celeriac pancakes *May be made in the morning for the evening, and reheated in the oven.*

*1 saddle of venison,
approx. 1.5kg in weight
(see Planning ahead)*
2 tablespoons groundnut oil
salt and pepper
15g butter

FOR THE SAUCE:

*the bones from the saddle
(approx. 900g in weight),
finely chopped*
100ml groundnut oil
*1 onion, peeled and
roughly chopped*
100ml port
*100ml Brown Chicken Stock
(see page 76)*
strained liquid from the morels
2 tablespoons whipping cream
*1 teaspoon arrowroot or
cornflour dissolved in
2 tablespoons water*

MAKING THE SAUCE

Preheat the oven to 200°C/400°F/Gas 6.

Heat the groundnut oil in a roasting tray until it reaches smoking point. Add the bones and roast in the preheated oven for 5 minutes. Add the onion and roast for a further 20 minutes until the onion is well coloured. Remove from the oven, drain off the fat, and transfer the venison bones to a saucepan.

Pour the port into the roasting tray and scrape off all of the caramelised juices on the bottom. Pour over the bones, then add the brown chicken stock, the liquid from the morels and the whipping cream. If there is not enough liquid to cover the bones add a little water. Bring all of this to the boil, skim and simmer for approximately 20 minutes. Pass it through a fine sieve, bring back to the boil, then thicken with the dissolved arrowroot.

Season to taste with salt and pepper and set aside.

MAKING THE POTATO AND CELERIAC GALETTE

Preheat the oven to 180°C/350°F/Gas 4.

Mix the grated potatoes with the grated celeriac, and season with salt and pepper.

Heat a medium non-stick pan with the groundnut oil until it reaches smoking point. Add the potato and celeriac mixture and pat it down firmly with a palette knife. Cook for 1 minute, then add the butter. Cook for a further minute, then turn and cook the other side for 2 minutes and place in the preheated oven for 5 minutes.

Remove from the oven, transfer the galette on to a wire rack and set aside.

COOKING THE VENISON

Preheat the oven to 180°C/350°F/Gas 4.

Heat a medium pan with the groundnut oil. Season the pieces of venison well with salt and pepper, then put in the pan. Brown for 1 minute, then add the butter and fry for a further minute, then cook in the preheated oven for 5-6 minutes. Remove from the oven and discard the fat. Leave to rest in a warm place for 5 minutes.

FINISHING AND SERVING

Cut the braised celery into slices as thinly as possible, then arrange it around four plates in a flower pattern. Keep warm. Drain the morels well.

Fry the bacon, morels and celery or parsley leaves for 1 minute in the hot oil. Set aside.

WINE

The richness of the venison requires a rich, warm and spicy wine; a good Shiraz from Australia, from a mature vintage, will be best.

FOR THE POTATO AND CELERIAC GALETTE:

250g peeled, washed and grated potato, squeezed dry in a dishcloth

150g grated celeriac

50ml groundnut oil

50g butter

TO SERVE:

Braised Celery (see page 140)

50g dried morels, soaked in 200ml water for 2 hours

150g streaky bacon, cut in 1cm strips

20 small celery or flat-leaf parsley leaves

1 tablespoon groundnut oil

Cut the galette into four and reheat it in the oven with the venison.

Heat the sauce and spoon it around the plate. Cut the venison fillets in half and place in the middle of the plates on top of the pieces of galette. Spoon the sauce around and decorate with the morels, bacon and celery leaves. Serve.

VARIATION

The galettes can be made in individual small pans. This is more time-consuming, but very effective.

RB'S NOTE

❧ *Venison cooked in this way is rare to medium rare. If you like it more cooked, add a few minutes to the cooking time.*

PEARS AND FIGS IN SPICED WINE
WITH CINNAMON CREAM

For 4 people

Planning ahead: *Everything can and indeed must be done ahead of time. The dessert can even be plated before you serve your starter, just leaving the sauce and cream to be put on at the last moment.*

4 firm but not hard Conference or Comice pears, peeled and cored

6 figs

1 orange, peeled and sliced as thinly as possible

FOR THE SPICED WINE:

100g blackcurrants, either frozen or bottled

100g caster sugar

200ml full-bodied red wine

2 cloves

2 juniper berries

½ cinnamon stick

2 bay leaves

2 tablespoons crème de cassis

FOR THE CINNAMON CREAM:

100ml whipping cream, whipped just to thicken slightly with 1 tablespoon caster sugar

½ cinnamon stick, grated on the finest part of your grater

POACHING THE PEARS AND FIGS

Cut a little slice off the bottom of each pear, so that they stand up straight.

In a medium saucepan, mix together the spiced wine ingredients. Add the pears to this and pour in just enough water to cover them. Top this with a round of greaseproof paper and then a weight to ensure that the pears remain submerged. Bring to the boil, then simmer gently for 30-40 minutes, depending on the ripeness of the pears.

Add the figs to the pears in the liquor and leave to cool. Once the pears and figs have cooled, transfer them and the orange slices on to a flat dish. Halve 2 of the figs.

FINISHING THE SAUCE

Reduce the poaching liquor until it becomes syrupy in texture, then pass through a fine sieve into a bowl. Allow to cool.

MAKING THE CINNAMON CREAM

Mix the whipped cream with the cinnamon and set aside.

SERVING

Arrange the pears on four large plates, with the whole figs alongside on top of an orange slice, and the half figs. Spoon the sauce over everything. Cover the whole figs with a little of the cinnamon cream, and serve. The bay leaves and cinnamon stick from the spiced wine may be used to garnish the dish.

RB'S NOTE

The sauce *You will probably be left with too much. This would make an interesting base for a Champagne cocktail.*

WINE

Either finish off the Shiraz with the pears, or try something like a late-harvest Riesling from Australia or California.

TABLE CANDLES

*Obviously candles can be
inserted in candlesticks if
you have them: decorate these
further with a suitable bow
(if appropriate and safe), and
with baubles and spray-painted
nuts around the foot of the
candlesticks. You can do
interesting things with groups
of candles. Large and fat church
candles that will stand easily
by themselves are particularly
useful; try and get them in
varying widths and heights.
You can surround them with an
appropriately sized ring which
you could have decorated in a
variety of ways – with fresh
foliage and flowers, pasta, nuts
or corks (see pages 67, 83, 123
and 55).*

MENU 12

*This Christmas buffet brunch is a feast for family and
friends that involves a fair amount of work beforehand,
but which leaves you with almost nothing to do at the
last minute. So enlist a little help in the days leading up
to your party, and just indulge on the day.
The salad recipes given here are for 4 small starter-size
portions, so make more or less, depending on how many
salads and people you are serving. The ham will serve
10-12 generously, the turkey 6-8, and the lobsters 4-8.
But all this is up to you and your guests, who may want
to go back to the table more than once!*

GLAZED HAM,
POACHED CROWN OF TURKEY,
BOILED LOBSTER

COUSCOUS WITH
CHICKPEAS AND VINE LEAVES,
CARROT, RAISIN AND
CHERVIL SALAD,
SALAD OF CURLY ENDIVES,
ROCKET, BACON AND
CROÛTONS, SALAD OF
CHICORY, STILTON AND
WALNUTS

MAYONNAISE, OLIVE OIL
VINAIGRETTE

TARTE AU CHOCOLAT

GLAZED HAM

For 10-12 people

Planning ahead: The ham may have to be pre-soaked (ask your butcher for how long). It may be cooked 3 days before, then cooled and kept in its liquid. Glaze a day in advance.

1 horseshoe gammon (topside and silverside), weighing approx. 6kg, rolled and tied (see Planning ahead)

2 onions, peeled and chopped

2 carrots, peeled and chopped

1 bouquet garni (thyme, bay leaf and parsley)

10 black peppercorns

10 cloves

FOR THE GLAZE:

50g cloves

100ml port

100g honey

3 tablespoons muscovado or other brown sugar

COOKING THE HAM

Place the ham in a large saucepan and cover with water. Add the onion, carrot, bouquet garni, black peppercorns and cloves. Bring to the boil and cook just below simmering point for 3 hours. Remove from the water and place on a wire rack to drain.

GLAZING THE HAM

Preheat the oven to 200°C/400°F/Gas 6.

With a sharp knife cut off the top layer of skin, leaving as much fat as possible. Cut a criss-cross pattern over the fat and put a clove in the middle of each diamond.

Bring the port and honey to the boil together in a small saucepan, then pour over the top of the ham. Rub in the muscovado sugar and glaze in the preheated oven for approximately 20 minutes. Keep a close eye on the ham whilst it is glazing: often ovens will cook more quickly towards the back, so it may need to be turned from time to time. Leave to cool.

RB'S NOTE

You could cook a slightly larger whole ham on the bone in the same way – it will indeed be more flavoursome closer to the bone. But with horseshoe gammon you get the best part of the ham, and it is much easier to carve and serve. The disadvantage, of course, is not having that lovely bone to make soup with afterwards.

POACHED CROWN OF TURKEY

This is a lovely way to poach turkey, very simple and a great presentation. A crown of turkey is the double breast taken off the bone; the wings can be left on.

For 6–8 people

Planning ahead: *Poach the evening or morning before.*

In a large pan, cover the crown of turkey with water. Add the salt, bring to the boil and skim. Cover with a round of greaseproof paper and simmer for 1¼ hours. Check if the turkey is cooked by inserting a skewer just underneath the wing bone. If it comes out hot and not followed by any blood, the crown is cooked. Leave to cool in the cooking liquor.

Remove from the liquor. Take the skin off and discard just before serving. Serve with some freshly made mayonnaise or vinaigrette.

RB'S NOTE

Keep and freeze the cooking liquor to use as a base for soups, either as it is, or reduced.

WINE

As it is Christmas, what else but Champagne! However, it might be better to choose one of the more vinous styles, such as the 'rich' cuvée produced by Veuve Clicquot.

1 crown of turkey,
weighing approx. 2kg

water to cover

1 tablespoon salt per litre
of water

NUT RING WITH CANDLES

Using the same type of ring frame as for the pasta (or cork) ring, use a glue gun to stick mixed nuts – Brazils, walnuts, almonds, hazelnuts etc – all over the frame. Use moss or broken pieces of nut to fill in any gaps. If you wish, you can spray the whole nut frame when finished, or you can spray a few nuts before gluing them on to the frame, to have a variegated effect. This could be hung, like the pasta or cork rings, but it also makes a good table decoration, with the middle filled with candles. Remember to put a plate or piece of card underneath to catch the candle drips.

BOILED LOBSTER

For 4-8 people

Planning ahead: The lobsters are best cooked on the day as needed, but will keep (cooked) in the fridge under a tea towel and some ice for 1 day.

4 x 750g live lobsters

Kill the lobsters by inserting the blade of a sharp strong knife between their eyes.

To cook the lobsters, just bring some water to the boil in a pot large enough to hold the lobsters. Boil them for 8-10 minutes, refresh immediately in cold water, then cool and refrigerate until needed.

Serve with mayonnaise or, if you prefer, some wonderful fruity extra virgin olive oil.

RB'S NOTE

When cooking live lobsters you do not need to salt the water as they seem to carry enough to season themselves.

COUSCOUS WITH CHICKPEAS AND VINE LEAVES

For 4 people

Planning ahead: This salad may be prepared at least a day ahead, adding only the parsley at the last minute.

COOKING THE CHICKPEAS

Drain the chickpeas and rinse them well. In a deep saucepan, cover them with water. Bring to the boil, then simmer for 1 hour. Check that they are cooked: they should be firm but tender. Drain and then place in a bowl with the olive oil to marinate. Season with salt and pepper.

STEAMING THE COUSCOUS

Steam the couscous for 10 minutes over simmering water, then mix well with the chickpeas and olive oil. Add the lemon juice and set aside.

COOKING THE VINE LEAVES

Heat a large frying pan with the groundnut oil until it reaches smoking point. Carefully place the vine leaves in and fry them for 30 seconds each side. Transfer to absorbent kitchen paper.

SERVING

Toss the parsley leaves with the couscous and chickpeas. Season well with salt and pepper to taste, decorate with the vine leaves, and serve.

100g chickpeas, soaked for 24 hours in 200ml water

100ml olive oil

salt and pepper

150g couscous, soaked in 150ml water for 30 minutes

juice of 2 lemons

50ml groundnut oil

12 vine leaves (these can be bought brined in most delis), patted dry

1 large bunch flat-leaf parsley, washed and picked

CARROT, RAISIN AND CHERVIL SALAD

For 4 people

Planning ahead: This salad will benefit from up to a day marinating in the vinaigrette.

Whisk the red wine vinegar and olive oil together. Season well, then add the raisins and grated carrot. Mix all together well, taste and season more if necessary. Add the chervil at the last minute.

600g carrots, peeled and grated (approx. 400g final weight)

100g raisins

1 bunch fresh chervil

1½ tablespoons red wine vinegar

75ml extra virgin olive oil

salt and pepper

SALAD OF CURLY ENDIVES, ROCKET, BACON AND CROÛTONS

For 4 people

Planning ahead: All of the ingredients can be prepared up to a day in advance and just mixed at the last minute.

1 head curly endive, prepared

50g rocket, prepared

100g streaky bacon, cut into lardons and fried

4 slices of white bread, cut into 1cm dice

Olive Oil or Groundnut Oil

Vinaigrette (see opposite)

Preheat the oven to 150°C/300°F/Gas 2.

Scatter the cubed bread on an oven tray, and place in the preheated oven for 20 minutes until completely dry and golden brown. Leave to cool.

Mix all the salad ingredients together, and serve with either an Olive Oil or Groundnut Oil Vinaigrette on the side.

SALAD OF CHICORY, STILTON AND WALNUTS

For 4 people

Planning ahead: This salad may be made 1-2 hours in advance but not too much longer as it will discolour.

800g chicory (approx. 6 large heads)

juice of ½ lemon

180g shelled walnuts

100g Stilton or other blue cheese, crumbled

Mustard and Hazelnut Dressing (see page 82)

Wash the chicory well, and discard any browning outer leaves. Shred the leaves slightly on the bias until you reach the hard core. Discard this. Sprinkle with lemon juice.

Toss the shredded chicory with the walnuts and blue cheese. Serve with the mustard and hazelnut dressing.

MAYONNAISE

Makes enough for 4 lobsters or 1 turkey crown

Planning ahead: May be made 2-3 days in advance.

Whisk together the egg yolks, mustard, 2 pinches of salt and 3 turns of pepper in a round-bottomed bowl. Add about 150ml of the oil in a slow trickle, whisking continuously, until the oil is absorbed, and the mixture turns pale yellow and thickens.

Loosen the consistency with the vinegar and lemon juice, then whisk in the remaining oil. Taste and season as necessary.

2 egg yolks, size 3
1 teaspoon Dijon mustard
salt and pepper
250ml groundnut oil (or half groundnut and half olive oil)
1 teaspoon white wine vinegar
juice of 1 lemon

OLIVE OIL VINAIGRETTE

Makes enough to dress 2 Salads of Curly Endives

Planning ahead: May be made weeks in advance.

Mix all the ingredients together, seasoning to taste.

RB'S NOTES

❧ *You could make this vinaigrette with groundnut oil instead of the olive oil. Use 80ml, not 100ml.*

❧ *Both of the vinaigrettes can be varied in many different ways, adding herbs, chopped shallots, a little diced fresh chilli, a clove of garlic or whatever you desire. The one thing to remember at all times is that a vinaigrette exists to complement and enhance the salad, not to overpower it. Always add a little less than you think necessary, then continue bit by bit until it is to your taste.*

100ml extra virgin olive oil
20ml white wine vinegar, or juice of ¼ lemon
salt and pepper

TARTE AU CHOCOLAT

For 8 people

Planning ahead: *The tart can be prepared half a day in advance.*

150g best cooking chocolate
50g unsalted butter, in pieces
50ml whipping cream
7 egg whites, size 3
60g caster sugar
5 egg yolks, size 3
50g plain flour
30g unsweetened cocoa powder
extra butter and flour for
the pastry ring

FOR THE WALNUTS:
100g walnuts, roughly chopped
icing sugar

**FOR COATING THE
TARTE:**
150g plain chocolate
50ml milk

Preheat the grill to its hottest. Preheat the oven to 180°C/350°F/Gas 4.

PREPARING THE WALNUTS
Place the chopped walnuts on a baking tray, sprinkle lightly with icing sugar, and grill for 1 minute. Reserve.

PREPARING THE PASTRY RING
Place a 28cm x 3cm pastry ring on a baking sheet. Butter the inside of the ring and the baking sheet base, and sprinkle with flour. Shake off the excess flour.

PREPARING THE CHOCOLATE MIXTURE
Melt the chocolate in a warm bain-marie. When the chocolate has melted, stir in the butter pieces with a spatula until they are totally incorporated and the mixture is smooth. Stir in the cream and remove from the heat.

In a mixing bowl, whisk the egg whites until they reach soft peaks, adding the caster sugar gradually, then stir in the egg yolks. Sprinkle in the flour and cocoa powder. Fold in the chocolate and butter mixture and mix slowly with a spatula.

COOKING THE TART
Pour half of the chocolate mixture into the pastry ring, sprinkle the walnuts in the middle, and then add the remaining chocolate mixture. Bake in the preheated oven for 12-15 minutes.

Remove from the oven and leave to cool for at least 10 minutes. Turn the tart out carefully on to a cooling rack and rest for at least 1 hour.

FINISHING AND SERVING
Place the rack on a tray. Melt the chocolate in a bain-marie and thin down with the milk. Spread the chocolate over the tart with a spatula and leave to cool for about 10 minutes.

With two spatulas, lift the tart and place it on a large round plate. Serve.

VARIATIONS
To simplify the tart, you could omit the chocolate coating and instead sprinkle it with icing sugar.

Sliced poached pears can be placed into the mixture instead of walnuts.

You could make chocolate shavings and surround the tart with them as in the photograph.

RB'S NOTE
Make sure the bain-marie does not boil, otherwise the chocolate will cook and become granular.

TABLE SWAGS

These are made in much the same way as garlands (see page 67). Fix the ends to the corners of the table with staples or heavy-duty drawing pins, and arrange little bows or arrangements at the corners. A table swag could be made to sweep into semi-circles, perhaps two from one end of the table to another. Here the material is completely artificial, using leaves, bows and gold baubles.

To Alex
from
Raymond

GIFTS FROM THE KITCHEN

These days the spirit of Christmas tends to get a little lost in the commercial madness leading up to it. I for one would prefer to know that, rather than plucking an item from the supermarket shelf, someone had spent a little time and care in their kitchen on a home-made gift. So here are a few ideas for you.

Try to find interesting jars and bottles in which to present these edible gifts, and you can go to town on the labelling. Either buy or make attractive labels to stick on the gifts, or buy or make labels you can tie on with ribbon or card. Use up pretty pieces of fabric for the tops, cutting the edges with pinking shears.

SHIITAKE AND
BUTTON MUSHROOMS
PRESERVED IN OIL

*These are a wonderful accompaniment to salads, pâtés or
as part of an antipasto.*

Fills 1 x 1 litre preserving jar

500g button mushrooms

500g shiitake mushrooms

white wine vinegar to cover (approx. 500ml)

1 teaspoon white peppercorns, crushed

1 teaspoon coriander seeds, crushed

2 bay leaves

1 sprig thyme

1 teaspoon salt

*extra virgin olive oil as required (100-150ml, plus more
to top up as necessary)*

BLANCHING THE MUSHROOMS

Wash the button mushrooms and then the shiitakes. Pat both dry
and keep them separate.

Bring the vinegar to the boil with the peppercorns, coriander
seeds, bay leaves, thyme and salt. Add the button mushrooms and
cook at a fast simmer for 2 minutes. Transfer them from the
cooking liquor on to absorbent paper.

Bring the vinegar back to the boil, drop in the shiitake
mushrooms and repeat the above process. Leave both sets of
mushrooms to cool completely.

BOTTLING THE MUSHROOMS

Prepare a large litre sterilised jar.

Put on a pair of clean plastic gloves and place in the shiitake
and button mushrooms, alternating them, making a sort of
checkerboard design. (This looks very effective but is time

consuming.) Alternatively you could just mix the mushrooms and
spoon them into the jar.

Cover the mushrooms with olive oil to the brim of the jar, and seal.

RB'S NOTES

 *As the mushrooms absorb the oil and the small cracks between
the mushrooms are filled you will probably need to add more oil.
The mushrooms must at all times be covered with oil or they will
turn sour. If you pay careful attention to this, the mushrooms should
keep for about 2 months in a cool dark larder.*

*The cooking liquor may be passed through a muslin cloth and
re-used.*

SPICED VINEGARED PEPPERS IN OIL

Fills 2 small jars

3 red peppers (approx. 600g), peeled and seeded

3 yellow peppers (approx. 600g), peeled and seeded

200ml white wine

100ml white wine vinegar

2 small fresh chillies, seeded and finely chopped

1 teaspoon salt

200ml olive oil, plus a little more to top up as necessary

Cut the peeled and seeded peppers into even strips.

Divide the white wine, vinegar, chillies and salt between two
separate pans, and bring to the boil. Put the red peppers in one
pan, the yellow in the other. Boil and then simmer for 6-8 minutes
until soft. Transfer from the pans to absorbent kitchen paper and
leave to cool.

Prepare 2 sterilised jars and line them with some of the pepper
strips. Fill the centres with the remaining peppers, and cover with
oil. Seal and store in the fridge.

RB'S NOTES

The peppers *They must at all times be completely submerged in oil or they will sour. If properly sealed, they will keep for up to 2 weeks in the fridge.*

 The cooking liquor *This may be kept and filtered, then used to make a wonderful vinaigrette for salads or a dressing for fish or scallops.*

KUMQUATS IN SYRUP

These are lovely little fruits that look stunning when preserved, even more so if you put some of the leaves into the jars. They make great petits fours and an interesting accompaniment to game dishes.

Fills 1 x 750ml jar

500g kumquats, well washed and patted dry
500g caster sugar

Place the kumquats and sugar in a deep pan together with just enough water to cover. Slowly bring to the boil and simmer gently for 10 minutes. Remove from the heat and leave to macerate in the syrup for 24 hours.

Return to the heat and slowly bring back to the boil, adding a little more water if necessary. Once again, remove from the heat and leave to stand in the syrup for 24 hours.

Bring the syrup slowly back to the boil, then remove the kumquats with a slotted spoon, letting as much syrup as possible drip back into the pan. Boil and skim the syrup for 5 minutes, then return the kumquats to the syrup and leave to stand for a further 24 hours.

Return slowly to the boil once more, then pour the syrup and kumquats into a sterilised jar, and seal very well.

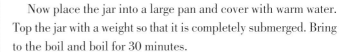

Now place the jar into a large pan and cover with warm water. Top the jar with a weight so that it is completely submerged. Bring to the boil and boil for 30 minutes.

Run warm water over the top, then lukewarm, then cold until the kumquats and jar are completely cold. Store in a cool dark place for up to 2 months.

PEARS IN SPICED WINE

8 firm but not hard Conference pears, peeled and cored

FOR THE SPICED WINE:

400g caster sugar
400ml full-bodied red wine (i.e. Bulgarian Cabernet Sauvignon)
6 cloves
6 juniper berries
zest of 1 lemon and 1 orange
1 cinnamon stick
2 bay leaves
100ml crème de cassis

In a large saucepan combine the sugar, red wine, cloves, juniper berries, citrus zests, cinnamon stick, bay leaves and crème de cassis.

Add the pears to this, then enough water to just cover, and top with a round of greaseproof paper. Follow with a weight to ensure that the pears remain submerged. Bring the lot to the boil and simmer gently for 30-35 minutes, depending on the ripeness of the pears.

Transfer the pears very gently with a slotted spoon to a large sterile jar, cover with the liquid and sterilise in the same fashion as the kumquats.

BLOOD ORANGE AND FIG WINE

A lovely fresh aperitif with a slightly unusual flavour. It's best made in a preserving jar so that the figs may be left whole.

Makes about 1.5 litres
100g zest and pith of blood orange
150g fresh whole black figs, washed and patted dry
200g caster sugar
2 bottles dry white wine

Cut the zest and pith of the blood oranges into 5mm strips. Mix these and the figs with the sugar. Spoon carefully into a jar and cover with the white wine. Seal and leave to macerate for at least a week.

Serve well chilled.

BLACKCURRANT LIQUEUR

Just the thing to drink after a splendid Christmas dinner, but it makes a very good gift as well.

Makes about 1.5 litres

500g ripe blackcurrants, washed and drained
1 litre tequila
300g caster sugar
1 clove
a few blackcurrant leaves (optional)

Crush the blackcurrants with a fork, and place them in a jar with the remaining ingredients. Seal the jar well, and leave to macerate in a cool dark place for at least 2 months.

Filter into a container, and then store in a sealed bottle.

FLAVOURED VINEGARS

Very simple to make, wonderfully decorative and often contribute that extra dash of something that you need to liven up a vinaigrette or marinade. These are more suggestions than recipes and must be treated as such. You are free to add or leave out an ingredient as fancy takes you. The vinegars may be made either in jars or bottles.

PROVENÇAL VINEGAR

Bay leaf
Thyme
Garlic
Rosemary
Sage
Peppercorns
Orange peel
Fresh chillies
A few sprigs of lavender
White wine vinegar to cover

SINGLE HERB VINEGARS

Rosemary and orange peel – White wine vinegar to cover
Tarragon and garlic – White wine vinegar to cover
Lemongrass and ginger – White wine vinegar to cover

VEGETABLE ACCOMPANIMENTS

—

Here I give you a selection of vegetable dishes which are truly seasonal. All of them are very simple, and since you are bound to be busy at this time, all are able to be prepared in advance. There are no strict rules about which vegetable accompaniment should go with which dish. For example, I would adore the mashed potatoes on page 141 with the very saucy game pie on page 38, but you may prefer the slight sweetness of the roasted Jerusalem artichokes (page 138). It is in your hands!

The recipes I have given are all for generous amounts if only serving one vegetable, even more so if serving two.

There you are – the spirit of Christmas.

BUTTERED BRUSSELS SPROUTS WITH BACON AND ALMONDS

For 4 people

Planning ahead: The Brussels sprouts *May be blanched and refreshed, then reheated with the bacon, almonds and butter at the last moment.*

500g small firm Brussels sprouts, bases and all withered leaves removed
salt and pepper
100g streaky bacon, cut into fine strips
20g butter
50g slivered almonds

Cook the Brussels sprouts in plenty of boiling salted water for 5-6 minutes. While they are cooking, pan-fry the bacon in a large frying pan.

Drain the Brussels sprouts in a colander, then add them to the pan with the bacon followed by the butter. Melt to give the sprouts a shine, then toss in the almonds. Season with salt and pepper, and serve.

GRATIN OF TURNIPS

For 6 people

Planning ahead: *This dish can be prepared 1 hour in advance and kept warm, or 1-2 days in advance, then topped with a little butter and reheated in the oven.*

700g turnips, peeled and thinly sliced
350ml whipping cream
½ bay leaf
1 sprig thyme
3 white peppercorns, crushed
1 garlic clove, peeled
a dash of white wine vinegar
salt

Preheat the oven to 180°C/350°F/Gas 4.

Boil the cream with the bay leaf, thyme, peppercorns, garlic, vinegar and a pinch of salt for 3 minutes.

Arrange the sliced turnips overlapping in a 20cm sauté pan. Strain the cream over them and press down. Cook in the preheated oven for 20 minutes, then serve.

BRAISED RED CABBAGE

For 6 people

Planning ahead: *This is the sort of accompaniment
that just improves with time, thus is perfect when made 2-3 days
before and reheated when needed.*

1 red cabbage, approx. 1kg in weight
1 onion, peeled and finely chopped
2 apples, peeled, cored and coarsely chopped
450ml full-bodied red wine (i.e. Spanish Cabernet Sauvignon)
50g stoned dates, very finely sliced
1 teaspoon caster sugar
1 teaspoon salt

Preheat the oven to 160°C/325°F/Gas 3.

Shred the red cabbage finely, then mix it together with the onion, apple, red wine, dates, sugar and salt in a heavy casserole dish. Cover and cook for 3 hours in the preheated oven. Stir from time to time and check after 2 hours.

When cooked the cabbage will be soft, sweet and melt in the mouth. There will be some liquid left in the pan; be sure to keep this, as when you reheat the cabbage it will reduce, thus concentrating the flavours and glazing the cabbage. Leave to cool and refrigerate until needed.

CAULIFLOWER PURÉE

For 4 people

Planning ahead: *The purée May be prepared up to 2 days in advance
and reheated slowly over a bain-marie. Alternatively it could be made
1-2 hours before the meal and kept warm under clingfilm.*

500g cauliflower florets, well washed with most of the stalks removed
salt and pepper
300ml whipping cream
150g butter

Preheat the oven to 180°C/350°F/Gas 4.

Cook the cauliflower in lots of boiling salted water until it becomes very soft, approximately 15 minutes. Strain into a colander and place this on a tray in the oven for 5 minutes.

In the meantime, heat the cream and melt the butter. Purée the cauliflower, cream and butter in a blender, then season to taste. Serve.

RB'S NOTE

If the cauliflower is not dried in the oven the resulting purée will be too liquid.

ROASTED JERUSALEM ARTICHOKES

For 4 people

*Planning ahead: The artichokes May be roasted 2-3 hours
in advance, then reheated in foaming butter. Alternatively,
if you were serving them with the roast turkey or goose, you could
just put them in the roasting tray 40 minutes before the end of the
cooking time and turn them every 10 minutes or so.*

*700g Jerusalem artichokes, peeled, washed and halved resulting in
half-barrel shapes about 6cm long, 3cm thick*

50ml groundnut oil

25g unsalted butter

salt and pepper

Preheat the oven to 180°C/350°F/Gas 4.

Heat the groundnut oil in a pan until smoking. Add the
Jerusalem artichokes and toss for 2 minutes. Add the butter, then
roast in the oven for 35-40 minutes, turning occasionally. Once
cooked the artichokes will be a rich caramel colour on the outside
and have a moist squishy interior. Season to taste and serve.

PAN-FRIED PARSNIPS WITH
ITALIAN PARSLEY

For 4 people

*Planning ahead: The parsnips May be cooked up to the
point where the parsley is added 2-3 hours in advance, then reheated
when needed, adding the parsley at the last minute.*

*600g parsnips, peeled, halved lengthways,
washed and cut into 5mm slices*

50ml groundnut oil

25g unsalted butter

1 small bunch Italian parsley, leaves picked

salt and pepper

In a large frying pan, heat the groundnut oil until it is at smoking
point. Add the parsnips to the pan in an even layer. Toss for
approximately 7 minutes until softened and beginning to brown.
Now add the butter and toss a further 3 minutes. By this stage the
parsnips should have a beautiful golden brown exterior and be
soft inside. Drain off any excess fat and add the parsley leaves.
Season to taste and serve.

BRAISED LEEK AND ROCKET

For 4-6 people

Planning ahead: The leek mixture *May be made
a day or so ahead of time, then quickly heated, adding
the rocket at the moment of serving.*

1 small onion, peeled and thinly sliced
30g butter
*500g leeks, the tough green part removed, sliced down
the middle, washed and sliced into 3cm pieces*
6 cardamom pods, crushed and tied in a small muslin bag
salt and pepper
100g rocket, washed

Cook the sliced onion in the butter without colouring for 2 minutes in a saucepan. Add the leek and cover with water. Add the cardamom and ½ teaspoon salt, then boil rapidly until soft, about 10 minutes.

Add the rocket and boil for a further minute, just until it wilts. Season and serve.

VARIATION

Watercress could replace the rocket.

CARROTS WITH CUMIN

For 4 people

Planning ahead: The carrots *May be cooked
a day ahead of time, then reheated with just a
little water added to them.*

*3 large carrots, peeled, washed and cut into
1cm thick slices (approx. 500g, prepared)*
200ml water

50g unsalted butter
*1 teaspoon – 1 tablespoon caster sugar,
depending on sweetness of carrots (please taste)*
½ teaspoon cumin seeds
salt and white pepper

In a deep saucepan, bring all of the ingredients to the boil. Turn down the heat and simmer until the carrots are tender, about 10 minutes.

Finish the cooking over a fierce heat, stirring frequently, until all of the liquid has evaporated and the carrots have a lovely shine.

VARIATIONS

Turnips or swede can be cooked the same way or, as they have similar cooking times, you could do a mixture of the two.

BRAISED CELERY

For 4 people

Planning ahead: *The celery May be braised 2-3 days in advance and kept in its own juices and then reheated in them. It can also be kept warm for 1-2 hours, since it is not a vegetable that will easily overcook.*

*2 whole hearts of young celery,
trimmed to approx. 15cm*
½ small onion (approx. 50g), peeled and sliced
500ml Brown Chicken Stock (see page 76)
salt and pepper
½ teaspoon fennel seeds
juice of ¼ lemon

Remove all the tough outer sticks from the celery and wash the hearts well. Place in a casserole that will hold them in one layer. Add the onion, cover with the chicken stock and add ½ teaspoon salt, the fennel seeds and lemon juice. Bring all of this to the boil, top with greaseproof paper, and simmer until soft, approximately 1 hour, 10 minutes.

When serving just remove from the liquid, and season with a little freshly ground black pepper. Keep the cooking liquid.

RB'S NOTE

N *Keep all of the celery trimmings to make a wonderful soup. Cook well with the liquid from this recipe and a little milk. Purée in a blender, then pass through a fine sieve to remove all the strings.*

GRATIN OF PUMPKIN

This dish can also be served on its own.

For 6 people

Planning ahead: *The pumpkin purée Can be made in advance, covered with clingfilm, and refrigerated.*

400g ripe pumpkin flesh, seeded and cut into 2cm dice
3 tablespoons water
2 eggs, size 3, separated
10g caster sugar
50g Gruyère or Emmenthal cheese, finely grated
freshly ground pepper
juice of ¼ lemon
25g unsalted butter

COOKING THE PUMPKIN PURÉE

Place the diced pumpkin and the water in a saucepan, cover and cook for about 20 minutes; remove the lid and boil to evaporate the water. Leave to cool.

Mix together the egg yolks and sugar and whisk well for 2 minutes. Add the cool pumpkin purée and two-thirds of the cheese. Taste and season with pepper.

PREPARING THE EGG WHITES

Whisk the egg whites until they form soft peaks, then add the lemon juice. Season with pepper, then briskly whisk one-third of the egg white into the purée. Carefully fold in the remaining egg white. Taste and correct seasoning.

COOKING THE DISH AND SERVING

Preheat the oven to 180°C/350°F/Gas 4.

Butter an oval 24 x 30cm gratin dish with a little of the butter, then pour in the purée mixture and sprinkle with the remaining cheese. Dot with the remaining butter and bake in the oven for 15-20 minutes. Serve to your guests.

RB'S NOTES

 The pumpkin *It must be ripe to ensure a full flavour.*

 Salt *No salt is added to this dish because of the salt in the cheese.*

BRAISED CHESTNUTS

This is an ideal accompaniment for any game dish, and for certain meats such as pork and turkey.

For 4 people

24 fresh sweet chestnuts
400ml Brown Chicken Stock (see page 76)
1 small celery stalk
1 teaspoon caster sugar
salt and pepper

Preheat the oven to 240°C/475°F/Gas 9.

With the point of a small knife, score a ring all around each chestnut without piercing the flesh. Bake in the preheated oven for 15 minutes. Cool for a while, then loosen, remove and discard the shells and the brown skin around the chestnuts.

In a saucepan simmer the chestnuts, stock, celery, sugar, salt and pepper gently for 10-15 minutes. Remove the chestnuts with a slotted spoon on to a serving dish and serve to your guests.

RB'S NOTE

 Pan-fried segments of apple will be a good addition to the chestnuts.

MASHED POTATOES

The type of potato that is used will determine the quality of the purée. Belle de Fontenay is the very best potato, but King Edward is easily obtainable and produces a good purée.

For 4-6 people

Planning ahead: *Perhaps the only dish that needs to be cooked at the last minute.*

800g whole potatoes, peeled and washed
2 litres cold water
40g salt
100ml whipping cream
350-400ml milk
80g unsalted butter
salt and pepper

Quarter the potatoes and simmer gently in salted water until they are perfectly cooked. Drain in a colander, then purée them through a mouli into a casserole. Place the casserole on a medium heat and stir in the cream, the milk and finally the butter. Taste and season with salt and pepper. Serve.

VARIATION

Butter could be replaced by olive oil. Cream can be omitted if you want a lighter purée, and it will still be delicious.

RB'S NOTES

 Timing for cooking is difficult since this depends on the size of the potato. To see how well a potato is cooked use the tip of a sharp knife. The water must not boil, or the outside of the potato will be overcooked and crumbly.

INDEX